Family, Inc.

How to Manage Parents, Siblings, Spouses, Children, and In-Laws in the Family Business

By Larry and Laura Colin

The Career Press, Inc.
Franklin Lakes, NJ

Family, Inc.
Edited and Typeset by Gina Talucci
Cover design by The Design Works Group
Printed in the U.S.A. by Book-mart Press

To order this title, please call toll-free 1-800-CAREER-1 (NJ and Canada: 201-848-0310) to order using VISA or MasterCard, or for further information on books from Career Press.

The Career Press, Inc., 3 Tice Road, PO Box 687,
Franklin Lakes, NJ 07417
www.careerpress.com

Library of Congress Cataloging-in-Publication Data

Colin, Larry, 1959–
Family, Inc. : how to manage parents, siblings, spouses, children, and
in-laws in the family business / by Larry and Laura Colin.
p. cm.
Includes bibliographical references and index.
ISBN 978-1-56414-985-5
1. Family-owned business enterprises—Management. 2. Family corporations—Management. I. Colin, Laura. II. Title.

HD62.25.C645 2008
658'.02--dc22

2007050993

Dedication

Larry:

To Grandpa Sam, whose amazing courage positioned our family for reaching the American dream.

To my beloved father, George, whose warmth, love, and kindness is forever etched in my heart.

To my loving wife, Laura, who made this book a reality.

Laura:

To Alexander, Sean, and Larry—the loves of my life.

Contents

Acknowledgments

We would like to thank: Michael Alvear, developer of Blabber Mash.com, whose facility with words helped bring this book to life.

Robyn and Willy Spizman of The Spizman Agency, for helping develop the concept.

Our agent, John Willig, of Literary Services, Inc.

John Ward, PhD, professor and codirector of The Kellogg School Center of Family Enterprise, for his time and expertise.

Drew Mendoza, managing principal of The Family Business Consulting Group International, for some candid advice.

Joseph H. Astrachan, PhD, executive director of Cox Family Enterprise Center, for his expertise.

Robert Arogeti, Habif, Arogeti, and Wynne LLP, for all the doors that opened for us.

Mike Mullman and Fred Lipman, Blank Rome LLP, for their legal advice.

Marshal Steinman, Marks Panet, and Shron LLP, an old friend and advisor.

Who Are You in the Family Business?

Every family business is unique except for the people in them. The names might change, but the problems never do. So, welcome to Family Business Central Casting where familiar characters meet common conflicts. Tell us who you are in the family business and we'll tell you how to resolve your most pressing problems:

Dad the Decider

You're the entrepreneur who started the business or took charge and created the empire. You couldn't wait for the family to be part of what you created, but now you can't believe the squabbling and attitudes that distract you from the business. You never imagined that managing the family would be harder than managing the business. How do you turn the family from a business burden to a corporate asset?

Mom the CFO (Chief Family Officer)

You are supposed to be the glue that keeps the family together, but the family business keeps getting in the way. You're getting frightfully close to needing a seating chart at dinner to separate people from each other. As the designated peacekeeper, how do you save the family from the business and the business from the family?

The Hard-Charging Son

You joined Dad in the family business because you see the company for what it could be—not for what it is. Ambitious and fearless, you want to steer the bus, but Dad won't let go of the wheel. It feels as though you fight over everything, but, in reality, your biggest difference is about the pace of change. How do you get Dad comfortable enough to let you take over more of the business?

In-Laws Under the Influence

You're either the son-in-law who works in your wife's family business or a supportive spouse whose husband works in the business. If you're the son-in-law, how do protect yourself from being treated like a second-class citizen? If you're a supportive spouse, how can you be an effective advocate for your husband without alienating the rest of the family?

The Father With Farewell Paranoia

You know in your heart it's time to retire, but you just can't seem to let go. Partly you're worried about financial security, but the thing you're not telling anyone is that the business gave you purpose, stature, and a strong identity. What will happen to all that if you leave? Oh, and then there's that succession issue. Eeny, meeny, miny, mo. Who do you pick so the business will grow?

The Sibling Rivals

You feel like pulling your brother out of his office and beating him up in the parking lot. You think your sister has always been daddy's favorite. To keep the business together, you'll have to work together. You and your sibs are the team the family business is counting on. But can you count on each other?

Uncle Ben Marries...Again

Your relative's marital status changes with the weather. New spouses, old spouses, new kids, old kids–family harmony went out the window years ago. All the divorces and remarriages are taking a toll on the family business. So, how can you protect the company from the family's adventures in love?

The Savvy Sister With the Killer Resume

You didn't jump into the family business when you were offered a job years ago. Now, after working in the corporate world and having your own family, maybe it's not such a bad idea. Should you leave that high-powered job for the family business?

The Parent in a Pickle

Your kid isn't working out. He's a mistake magnet. Customers demand he be taken off the accounts and your staff thinks his title should be changed from VP of Sales to VP Who Fails. You're angry, but heartbroken. Is he a lost cause or can you turn him around? And if you can't, how do you handle the ultimate family business nightmare–firing your own child?

Mr. and Mrs. Inc.

You and your spouse are attempting to go where few have gone successfully–working together in a business. You'll either be a great team or wind up killing each other. You're trying to handle it all: complex business situations, the house, the kids, the dog, and maybe even an elderly parent. It's testing the outer limits of space and your relationship. Can you grow the business without shrinking your marriage?

The Perplexed Parent

You can't decide whether to sell the business or give it to the kids. Tough competition, looming retirement, and questions about the kids' competence are driving you nuts. Do you hand over the business to the kids and take the chance they'll scramble your nest egg? Or do you sell the business and take a chance they'll never speak to you again?

I am a 37-year veteran of an enormously successful family business. I started out by driving my grandfather to his business appointments and ended up as chairman of Colin Service Systems–a fourth generation, 92-year-old family business.

My story is typical of many Americans with immigrant parents or grandparents. At 10 years old, my grandfather was the first in his Polish family to board a ship for America (alone, no less). Without any family to comfort or protect him, he worked in a garment factory, then started a one-man window cleaning company. Two generations later, it had turned into a multi-service regional powerhouse with sales approaching $200 million.

As Grandpa got more clients, the family started working with him. Everyone got involved, and through the generations, we learned the basic values: teamwork, a strong work ethic, and taking responsibility. We had a shared sense of purpose. We were passionate about what we did. We worked six days a week and loved every minute of it. We polished our shoes on Sunday to be ready for Monday. We were a team–related by blood, unified by goals, and bound by passion.

As the company grew, we changed the name to Colin Service Systems and even started a new company, Effective Security Systems. Any family can have their name on a business card, but on a building? The entire family beamed with pride. We had hit the big time and could attract the terrific professional managers that made our company great. We got involved in social scenes, charity events, and political campaigns. There was hardly a door we could not open. We were even on Crain's List, one of New York's largest privately held companies.

Yet, with the success came the typical conflicts and growing pains that required changes we were not willing to make. Eventually, difficult relationships within the family took their toll on the business. I've learned there are three sides to every story about a family business failure–yours, theirs, and the truth. I've also learned that "being right" might save your ego, but it won't save the business.

For most of my working life, I considered our family business a jewel to pass on to the next generation, just as it had been passed on to me. But it wasn't meant to be. In the end, some of the family's relationships were irreparable. The only way out was to sell the company. At the closing, the lawyers told me to initial here and sign there, but my mind wasn't on the papers. It was on the phone call I had to make to my father after the sale. The call confirming the end of what he inherited from his father and what he had so proudly passed down to us.

After signing the legal agreements at the closing, our family would forever change. We would lose a part of our identity, our collective soul. Calling my dad after the closing was one of the toughest things I'd ever done. Every number I pressed quickened my pulse. When he picked up the phone a surge of shame and embarrassment washed over me. "It's done," I said. "Dad, I'm so sorry." His answer surprised me. I knew how disappointed he was with the way things turned out, so I expected some expression of regret. But that's not what happened. "You made me proud of you," he said. "We had a good run. We built a great company, created jobs, gave back to the community, and supported ourselves in the process. That isn't a failure–that's a success that ran its course."

That's why I loved my dad so much. I had called to comfort him and he comforted me! It's one of the reasons I had breakfast with him almost every day for 19 years. Despite his words of comfort, I couldn't help but feel the pain he must have felt. My father died a year after the company was sold at the age of 86.

The dream of continuing the family legacy was over, but another one took hold–this book. Since the sale of our family business, my wife Laura and I devoted ourselves to a single idea: helping other family businesses stay together so they'll never have to make the phone call I had to make to my father.

Laura and I have plenty of personal experiences to write this book. After earning her MBA and working as an investment banker, she joined our family business. But we wanted to strengthen our affect by studying the structure and challenges of other family businesses. So, we interviewed experts, family business executives, consultants, and business-school faculty. Our work confirmed what we intuitively believed–that our experiences were universal and that practical solutions exist.

Family, Inc. will help your family business grow and prosper by showing you how to recognize and resolve problems before they get too big to manage. With our collective experience, we will show you the three most important aspects of running a successful family business:

1. How to anticipate, understand, and resolve the most common issues in a family business.
2. How to deal with parents, siblings, and other family members.
3. How to avoid or neutralize the emotional fall out of business decisions and their effects on the family.

Family, Inc. isn't just for the head of the family business. It's for everyone in it, around it, or affected by it. Each chapter is devoted to a character unique to most family businesses. Choose your character and you'll see the distinct conflicts you face as a father, mother, brother, sister, or extended family. Written from your perspective, it's filled with useful advice to get you where you want to go.

Choose another character and you'll see some of the same problems from *their* perspective–and the advice we have for them. We want you to get inside the heads of other family members. Whether you choose to read about Dad the Decider, The Sibling Rivals, or The Hard-Charging Son, this format provides an engaging, effective way to understand the most common conflicts in a family business, the "characters" that cause them, and proven approaches to keeping the peace. *Family, Inc.* will give you a 360-degree view of what's going on and improve the odds of preventing a minor misunderstanding from developing into a major disaster.

My father used to tell us about the "Curse of the Plotnick Diamond." It was the biggest, most expensive diamond in the world, and available to any woman who wanted it. The curse of the Plotnick diamond was that Mr. Plotnick came with it. Companies run by relatives have their own curses, but it doesn't have to be that way. *Family, Inc.* will help you turn your curses into blessings and make that diamond a priceless gem your family will hand down from one generation to the next.

The gender references throughout this book are purely for illustrative purposes.

Chapter 1

Dad the Decider

'My family? Hell no, those are my clients'

Just about every family business has one: the father who either started the business or ascended to the throne. Either way, he has the power to bring you into the company or kick you out, to raise your salary or lower your expectations. We're calling him "Dad the Decider," because he's the guy who makes the final decisions on just about everything. He may have gotten to where he is by exercising absolute authority, but he can't get to where he wants without exercising restraint. His biggest frustration is that he'd rather run the business, not the family. But as the business grows, so does his family's involvement; the more family is involved, the more chance for conflict. He doesn't purposefully want to injure his family's relationships, but he's got a business to run.

If you're Dad the Decider, you'll appreciate that this is written from your perspective. If you're a family member dealing with Dad, the chapter will help you understand his thinking and deal with him more effectively. We'll start with a scenario that portrays Dad's struggles, then move on to helpful insights that show how he views the world. Finally, we'll provide a step-by-step action plan to increase Dad's chances of running a successful family business.

Dad the Decider's Dilemma: A Typical Scenario

How can I run a successful business and keep my family happy at the same time?

Our most profitable customer threatened to cancel our contract if he had one more problem. "Frankly, ever since your daughter took over the account," he said, "the service has gone downhill." Furious, I called my daughter in, demanding answers. All I got were excuses. So, there I was, stuck between the daughter I loved and the customer I needed. Well, I can't risk the business to spare her feelings. So I told her, "This is how we're going to fix it: I'm taking you off the account and putting your brother on it. You will take over his new college account."

She came unglued. "You've never had any confidence in me," she yelled. "You're going to give my brother my best account because you think I can't handle it. Dad, he doesn't even talk to me at the office. It's like we don't have the same last name!" She walks out in a huff slamming the door so hard the papers fly off my desk.

I go home and my wife's on me before I even shut the door. "What the hell did you say to our daughter?" she asks. "I am trying to save our best customer," I snapped. "Yes," she said, "And I am trying to save our family."

I decide to tell my son the plan first thing in the morning. As I walk in the office, I see he's in *my* conference room in a meeting with strangers–and he's sitting in *my* chair. I poke my head in and call him outside. "Who are these people and why are you in my conference room instead of your office?" "Oh, they're with a new insurance company I believe we should consider. They have several clients in our industry. I tried to tell you about them yesterday but you were too busy."

I stared at him in disbelief. "You have no authority to change anything in this company unless you clear it through me. And, why are you wasting time on this? Aren't you suppose to be following up on the list we discussed last week?" I marched into my office slamming the door, so furious, I forgot to tell him he'd be switching accounts with his sister.

I had looked forward to the day when the kids would join the family business, but it's creating more problems than I ever imagined–in the office and at home. They can't work together, and they challenge every decision I make. Worse, they think I should agree with every change they want. This company is my baby and it'll stay that way until I say so. Maybe the kids should work for someone else.

What's Dad Thinking?

Dad is caught in the crosshairs. Every time he wants to take care of business, the family gets in the way. He always dreamed his children would join him in the company, but the dream never included these kinds of distractions. He doesn't understand why working with his children has become such a battle.

In Dad's mind, the business needs responsible adults marching behind him. He's embarrassed by the kids' immaturity and uncertain if bringing them into the business was such a great idea. They're so wrapped up in themselves, they can't see the serious business issues in front of their faces, much less what's looming on the horizon. Dad lives in fear that the business he worked so hard to build will collapse under the weight of the family.

He's right. Studies show about 1/3 of family-owned businesses survive into the second generation. Only around 10 percent make it into the third. These are not exactly the odds you wanted to hear. Forewarned is forearmed, though, and nothing is more foreboding than this: Family-based issues are the greatest threat to Dad's company. The odds are against him if he doesn't take action.

Adding to the frustration, Dad's wife is fanning the flames of the conflicts. Home used to be a refuge, but now it's just an extension of the office. Dinner is increasingly becoming an interrogation session conducted by a hyper-vigilant mom. In the past, his wife had been his biggest supporter. In rough times and good times, she understood the importance of the business in their lives. But since the children joined him, she seems more interested in keeping the family peace than protecting the family business. Every night includes a review of each kid's workday, with Mom often taking sides and second-guessing Dad's decisions.

Dad never anticipated this. He believes the family should be grateful for the opportunity he's given them. Family firms provide benefits no other company can touch. Where else can Dad's children get the president of the company to be their personal mentor? What other place will give them this financial security and the opportunity to build a company that could eventually be theirs? Who will be more forgiving of their mistakes?

Looking back, Dad went through hard times that the kids can't even imagine. He remembers working through the night and most weekends, staying at lousy motels to fix a customer's problem. He lost sleep fearing the company might not make its loan payments. Today, the business is rock solid and he's earned his bragging rights.

Dad expects his kids to make the company their priority, too, but they haven't. Customer service, sales quotas, and professional conduct seem to take a back seat to power plays, sibling rivalries, and hurt feelings. Dad's not the only one distressed; there's an uncomfortable atmosphere for everyone at the office. Employees pick up on the family soap opera and each episode generates whispers and snickers at the water cooler.

Most Dads take predictable approaches to the family business squabbles. Some pretend the issues don't exist. Some hope they'll go away by themselves. Others, similar to the dad in our story, react by pulling rank and forcing the kids to comply.

Neither approach works. The head-in-the-sand method simply postpones the inevitable while the command and control method accelerates the resentment. That's why we've developed the following five Action Steps, based on our personal experiences, to help Dad keep the business on track once the family comes on board. If you're Dad, memorize these steps. If you're dealing with Dad the Decider at the office or at home, read our recommendations and determine how you can help Dad implement them.

Five Action Steps for Dad the Decider

Action Step #1

Pay as much attention to the family-driven issues as you would your customer-driven issues.

Make family management an important part of your business management. An ounce of anticipation is worth a pound of solution.

It sounds simple, right?

Not for you, Dad, or any other entrepreneurial businessman, for that matter. Every waking hour is devoted to selling and delivering service, making the product, and satisfying customers. That's where you feel compelled to spend 100 percent of your time. Sure, you care about the company's employees, but human resources hasn't been your focus. Who knew that once the kids arrived at the company, "family management" would be another responsibility taking time out of your jam-packed day?

Well, we can tell you it's your biggest responsibility. Our family business story would have a different ending if we had paid more attention to the troubles the family was brewing at the office. We understand it's easy to sweep aside family annoyances when you are in the middle of daily business disruptions, but if you don't circle back around to tackle it, expect the problems to come back even stronger. You will never have a thriving, solid family business if you don't manage the family as well as you do other aspects of your business.

We want you to treat your family-driven business issues as you would any customer's issues. Consider this: when a customer calls with a problem, you don't ignore it or ram the solution down his throat. In fact, you anticipate the problems before you get the complaint. You know that customer like you do the back of your hand, and you bring in the A team to consult with you when something's gone wrong. Together you develop solutions to the problem and a follow-up program to measure progress.

Once even one family member joins your business, it's time to kick family management into gear. That means paying pretty close attention to job performance and relationships with other family members and others. Let's go back to the story as an example: Using the same level of attention, how could the Dad in our scenario have headed off a choice between saving the account and saving his daughter's feelings? First, by acting, not reacting. Dad should have been regularly checking in with the client as soon as he put his daughter in charge of the account. A friendly call to see how the transition was going would have uncovered issues before they snowballed out of control. If problems developed, Dad could have met with his daughter and confronted the problem together. Step one was asking the right questions: Did she have a personality conflict with the customer? Was there a pattern to the customer service issues? Would teaching her how to delegate more effectively improve service? Dad should have been aiming for Daughter's buy-in. Then, if things didn't work out, Daughter at least would understand that it wasn't some arbitrary decision on Dad's part.

But what if it's too late? What if Dad didn't do his early homework and the problem really does come down to taking Daughter off the account or losing it? First, he should calmly explain the situation to her. Get on the side of the solution, not the problem. Ask her, "How can we save this account?" If she's smart, she'll offer to remove herself from the client. If she insists on staying, share stories of how you had to sacrifice an account (a bit of exaggeration never hurts) for the company's good. Be accessible to her throughout the next few weeks after you make the account change. The result may be the same (taking Daughter off the account), but the process isn't. Dad is much more likely to keep the relationship with his daughter intact and make her better at what she does if he brings her into the decision-making process.

How do you know when there's trouble lurking with the family at the company? Is there a way to uncover problems before they spiral out of control? Absolutely. Take a family member's temperature with a routine early breakfast or lunch, just to "check in." It should be a regular event, regardless of whether things are going smoothly. Don't come with an agenda or to-do list. Use the occasion to build bonds and give you a better chance to head off issues before they get unmanageable.

An International Example

In touch in Taiwan

At Taiwan-based Fubon Financial Holdings, the Tsai family banking tycoons still try to maintain high-touch communication between Dad Tsai Wan-Tsai and sons Daniel and Richard. They meet for lunch every Monday to discuss business, and the brothers, who live in the same apartment building, speak several times a day by phone or in person.

The Big Point

If a family member becomes a habitual no-show at your "check-ins" or other family social events, get to the bottom of it; they're avoiding the meetings for a reason.

The other Action Steps in this chapter will give you more ideas on what to do once the family has joined your company. Remember, a successful family business begins with successful family relationships. Make that part of your management responsibilities and you'll be on the way to creating the legacy.

Action Step #2

Change from Dad the Decider to Dad the Compromiser.

Chances are your decisions haven't been challenged in a long time. Time's up. If the company is growing, you need fresh ideas and energy. By bringing family into the business, you've put the welcome mat out and sent the signal that you value their input. Don't contradict yourself by thwarting new approaches, resisting change, and making everyone fearful of floating new ideas past you. You'll just lay the groundwork for later conflicts.

It's time to lose your Dad the Decider persona and introduce a compromising side to your management style. As you morph into Dad the Compromiser, create a forum where managers and family can openly express their views and feel as though they are a part of the decision-making. Sociologists report that people are most likely to support a decision, even when they disagree, if they have some say about it. That's why you should share the stage; you don't have to exit stage left, but you do need to allow a bigger cast in the performance.

- **Set up a leadership council.** By enlarging your inner circle to include top managers you'll open the floor to new ideas. Schedule monthly meetings and you'll discover what we did: The smartest people in the company didn't have our last name.
- **Share sensitive information.** Sharing confidential information with people who may not have the family name is a gesture of trust. Your staff will reward you with greater loyalty and better ideas.
- **Insist that everyone offers new ideas.** If you've been ruling with an iron fist, people will be too afraid to make suggestions, even if you invite them into inner circles. Ask for ideas. Insist on them. Pay close attention and implement them if they make sense. Make people feel as though they are a part of the process, not just receiving edicts from higher-ups.

As you step in and out of your roles as dad and boss, you need to complete the transition from Dad the Decider to Dad the Compromiser. You'll get a huge payoff when you show your new persona to the family. Consider it the art of changing your answers from an automatic "no" to a thoughtful "maybe."

On page 31, there are a few examples that really show how these ideas are put into action.

Finally, discuss with your family your challenge of wearing two hats of parent and boss. Tell them it will take time to perfect the new juggling act: getting your son's career back on track during the week, and then setting up his new barbeque on Saturday.

Problem	Dad the Decider	Dad the Compromiser
Son wants to introduce new cost-accounting software to track product profitability.	"We don't need it. It costs too much."	"Let's see a demonstration and show me how the benefit justifies the cost."
Daughter asks for managerial responsibilities that require people skills she doesn't have.	"What are you thinking? You know you're not good with people. Besides, they won't accept a young manager anyway."	"I like your ambition. Let's talk about the skills you'll need to make a successful manager and if you need training."
Nephew wants to make personnel changes that would make Dad's long-term employees obsolete.	"These people have been with me since the beginning. Now you want to throw them out on the street just because you're here?"	"Tell me what you believe is missing in their skill set and how it affects us. New directions are as important as old loyalties—let's see how we can bridge the gap."

Action Step #3

Don't try to solve all of the family business issues alone.

Hire a family business consultant. Your company lawyer or trusted accountant isn't equipped to handle the complicated psychological family dynamics that play out at work. Family business consultants are specialists, and they have seen and resolved many of the same problems you're experiencing now. The good ones will start with a "family audit," a systematic assessment of how the family intersects with the business. As an impartial third party, family business consultants can make recommendations on governance, sibling strife, communication, organization structure, and conflict resolution that take into account the business you're in and the family that's a part of it.

We're certain that hiring a consultant would have helped our own family business. We didn't do it then for the same reasons you're probably not doing it now: shame, embarrassment, ego, and concern about the cost. Dad the Decider may think, *"I don't want outsiders to see that my sons don't get along,"* or worse, *"I don't want anybody to see that I can't manage the family."* Dad probably doesn't want to hear what he already knows: his family is operating more like *The Sopranos* than *The Brady Bunch.*

Our advice: get over it and commit the funds. These consultants aren't paid to judge you; they're paid to help you diagnose and resolve the problems.

The Big Point

Where's the doctor? There's an entire broad-based industry of family business consultants and therapists who can integrate family personalities into your business. Here's how to find them:

- ➟ Click on the Family Firm Institute Website, *www.ffi.org.* For family businesses outside the United States, try Family Business Network, International, *www.fbn-i.org.*
- ➟ You can subscribe to *Family Business Magazine* and look in the Service section online at. *www.familybusinessmagazine.com*
- ➟ Go to school. Many local universities have a family business program and often host family business conferences that are well attended by consultants.

Action Step #4

Determine the "Rules of Engagement" before the family joins you in the business.

You have "rules of engagement" with your customers, don't you? It's called a contract. Why should your family be different? You need to document a clear understanding of expectations. Begin by jointly determining with your new family member the right job position that utilizes his or her strengths. You'll need something in black and white, something to which you can point, so decisions don't seem so arbitrary. Then sit down and review the rules. Here are the ones we should have used:

Start somewhere else

Encourage family members to work somewhere else before joining the family business. There's no better way to introduce the concepts of authority, accountability, and professional conduct than working elsewhere. Once they see the pervasive job insecurity in many companies and get a taste of being treated as someone who is about to be outsourced, they'll be grateful for the opportunity you offer them.

The Big Point

Don't Make It So Easy to Join the Club

Formalize entry into the family business with on-site orientations and a written list of expectations. Set minimum education and work experience requirements.

Pay market rates

Don't pay family more than the appropriate salary for the position. You'll feed an entitlement attitude that says who you are is more important than what you contribute. You can get an idea of salary ranges by looking at industry salary surveys, contacting employment agencies, and contacting head-hunting firms. Review resumes of people in similar positions.

Avoid paying your family members equally; this could be a recipe for disaster if, in time, the levels of responsibility become wildly different. Keep other perks such as expense accounts and company cars in line with the responsibility and position. Finally, establish a clear bonus program or dividend policy, separate from salary, when distributing profits of the business. If they hit the targets, they get the goods; if they don't, they hit the showers. Reward achievement, discourage entitlement.

You be the judge

Insist on formal performance reviews at least once per year. They may be family, but they're still employees. Formal reviews give you an opportunity to assess strengths, weaknesses, and their commitment to the business.

Performance reviews should include action plans, goals, and educational training for the coming year (computer training or a course in sales management or public speaking) with rewards for reaching them and penalties if they don't.

If other employees are involved in a family member's review, have the nonfamily member report only the hard data, not the evaluation. Did your son meet the sales quota? Did your daughter make the required number of customer service calls? The nonfamily member reports the data, you make the evaluation. This way you protect the non-family member and redirect the potential for resentment away from him.

Performance reviews also include attitude, respectfulness, and other hard-to-measure attributes. We doubt anyone will tell you that your son is an SOB and your daughter's no better. They're not going to risk alienating you or the family, so watch out for hints from employees trying to pass on important information. If you hear–or in some cases overhear–"Man, I've never seen a woman slam the phone down as fast or as hard as she does," you probably have a niece whose customer service skills need work. Or if you hear, "Boy, your son can drink anyone under the table," then he probably needs a lesson or two on setting boundaries, especially at dinner with conservative clients.

The Big Point

Use Reviews to Build Bonds, Not Walls

Be the loving coach looking out for the best interest of your family, not the stern critic who judges them harshly. Frame everything encouragingly: "I see a great future with you, and here's what we need to work on to make that possible."

Remind them that they're ambassadors, not just employees

Be candid about how you expect your family to conduct themselves on the job. As ambassadors of the business, tell them you're holding them to a higher standard than nonfamily members. You expect them to be the first ones in the office and the last ones out the door. Explain the need to be enthusiastic and helpful, and, really, a cheerleader for the business and its employees. Why? Because he who has his name on the door sets the tone in the room. She whose name commands attention is closely watched. Consistently showing up late and leaving early creates copycats *("Hey, if she can leave early why can't I?")* or resentfulness *("If the owner's son isn't putting in the hours, why should I?")*.

Don't avoid legal documents

Shouldn't family members be able to waltz into the business? Shouldn't your relationship be as casual in the office as it is in your home? No. No. NO. (Did we mention no?) When your family joins the company, you have to realize the people you love have the capacity to grow the business or bring it to its knees.

Signing legal documents is one of the most sensitive and contentious issues about joining the family business. No matter how diplomatically conducted, there's an unavoidable "us against them" feeling to the negotiations. We know it'll tear your heart out when your son says, "But Dad, don't you trust me?" But trust isn't the issue here–protection is. We know you can't conceive of a close family member taking employees and confidential information to set up a competing shop, but you can't take that chance. It happened to us, but, thankfully, the company was protected because we made everyone sign agreements.

Employment agreements and shareholder agreements establish the obligations of the company to an individual and the individual to the company. Here's a brief description of what they're about. See your lawyer for a more thorough discussion:

1. **Employment agreements.** They're a must. Every family member who joins the company's management should sign one. Here are the main subjects to address:
   - ➡ Job Responsibilities–Get the details. What are their titles, to whom do they report, what are the specific goals and responsibilities of the job?
   - ➡ Compensation–Spell it out. Salaries, incentives, health insurance, vacations–everything. Whatever you leave out may come back to haunt you, so be thorough.
   - ➡ Noncompete–Snuff it out. Do you want a family member taking everything they have learned from you and steal your customers? Then get a pen.

- Nondisclosure–Keep it shut. If loose lips sink ships, imagine what they'll do to your business. Consider this the blabbermouth clause. It keeps everyone from sharing your confidential information.
- Nonsolicitation–Close the gates. It keeps former employees from poaching current employees.
- Termination–The "go-away" clause. What are the grounds for being fired? What will the severance payments be? What if they resign?

2. **Shareholder's Agreement.** This is the most important legal document you can sign once you're an owner. Think of it as the "who gets what" document. As in, "Who gets what if I die, become disabled, leave the company, or want to cash in my shares?" Without a shareholder agreement, everything, and we mean everything, will probably end up in court. And if you're lucky enough to settle before The Robed One does it for you, those negotiations will not be nice. Picture this nightmarish scenario:
   - Your favorite aunt resigns and wants to cash out her 10 percent.
   - She says it's worth $125,000 and wants it by Friday.
   - You have no agreement stating the value of the stock or how it is to be paid.

You might as well put your lawyer on speed dial.

Your attorney can help you develop a proper shareholder agreement, but here are some main questions we think you need to consider:

- How do we determine what the shares are worth?
- If somebody wants to cash out when will the payments be made?
- What happens if the company can't make the payments?

It can take years for a court to decide on these types of questions, and, even then, those decisions might not go your way. Without a shareholder's agreement, the only right you have is to get a lawyer.

The Big Point

What's Love Got to Do With It?

How do you deal with family members who feel insulted about signing legal documents? First, recite the golden rule: Everybody signs. No exceptions, including you. That way nobody feels singled out.

Second, treat the business as a separate entity from the family. Talk about the business in the language of business. They're not dealing with "dad," they're dealing with a company, and the company has rules everyone obeys.

Third, use lawyers. Let the company's attorney deal with your family member's lawyer. They'll act as go-betweens–masters of 'conflict insulation' that protect the family from difficult face-to-face negotiations.

Action Step #5

Position the business as an opportunity of a lifetime.

In many family businesses, Dad the entrepreneur works hard as hell building the company, and, once successful, spoils the kids. When the kids join the business, Dad doesn't understand their attitudes. They tend to see it more as a personal ATM than a platform for prosperity. Do they understand they have to put a lot of work in before they can take any money out? Do they respect what you've accomplished? Do they understand how hard you and other family members have worked to get here? And here's the most important question of all: Do they have an entitlement mentality? Because if they do, and you let them in the company, we suggest you buy stock in Tylenol.

Here's how you know you have a family member with an entitlement mentality:

- Your son, the recent college graduate, wants a six-figure salary, a company car, and the same bonus you receive.
- Your nephew thinks every weekend is a three-day holiday.
- Your 22-year-old daughter wants to know why the general manager doesn't ask her opinion.
- Your niece, the administrative assistant, doesn't understand why her boss can't take her to the airport.
- Your son's wife comes into the office in her tennis outfit.

- Your daughter asks your assistant if she can type her child's term paper.
- Your son demands an increase in salary after a key manager left and he knows you're in a bind.

What can you do when a family member has an entitlement mentality? If they are in the business, you have to be tough. Put them on notice. If there's no improvement, show them the door. Invite them to get a job at other companies and get a taste of the real world. Remember, if you notice their attitude, your employees will too. You need to surgically remove the morale-busting perpetrator from the family business and let them grow up on someone else's watch.

They can knock, but you don't have to let them in

Let's say your spoiled niece, nephew, or cousin is begging to get hired. Should you? No. They'll always have a laundry list of demands that will create inequities in compensation and resentment among employees. To satisfy their entitlement hunger you'll have to give them things they don't deserve, which will create a pervasive "why can't I have the same thing" attitude across the company. Worse, the demands of the entitled always escalate. Do you really want to spend time meeting demands that are as unfair as they are insatiable?

Here's what you say when such a family member wants in: "I can't meet your expectations. I think you're better off working for an outside company." And if that doesn't work, try the direct route: "You're expecting too much out of your position. You're giving me the feeling that if I give you an inch, you're going to take a mile."

Respect, just a little bit

It should have happened when they were kids, around the dinner table when you discussed the daily happenings at the company or when they visited you at the office and saw how hard you worked. They should have felt the common mission, the struggle and desire to continue the family business. It all adds up to respect–respect for what the business means to the entire family.

If your family needs a little reminder, be sure to tell them about the priceless perks they can't get anywhere else. Whether it's part-time work for a daughter with children, or summer work for a college-bound cousin, the family business can be extraordinarily flexible and convenient in providing money and experience. Of course, the affect of the business on the family goes beyond just providing jobs. Because it, most likely, supports local charities, religious organizations, and civic events, the family name becomes a prestigious badge that opens social, civic, and business doors closed to others. Whether it's getting invited to A-list parties or official city functions, the business lends weight to the family name.

Chapter Summary

Dad the Decider

Remember, around 30 percent of family businesses survive into the second generation and 10 percent into the third. Follow these steps to beat the odds:

- **Action Step #1:** Treat your family-driven business issues as you would any customer's issues. You will never have a strong, solid family business if you don't manage the family as well as you do other aspects of your business.
- **Action Step #2:** Lose your Dad the Decider persona and introduce a compromising side to your management style. Create a forum where managers and family can openly express their views and feel as though they are a part of the decision-making.
- **Action Step #3:** Hire a family business consultant or therapist to help you navigate through the unique issues all family businesses face. Join a family business center at your local university.
- **Action Step #4:** Set rules of engagement for family joining the business. We suggest the following "musts":
    - Prior work experience.
    - Market rate salaries.
    - Periodic performance reviews.
    - Exemplary conduct as ambassadors for the business.
    - Appropriate legal agreements. Employment agreements and shareholder's agreements (when applicable).
- **Action Step #5:** Weed out entitlement mentalities by refusing to hire spoiled family members and firing them if they wreak havoc.

Mom the CFO

MY SON THE GENIUS
"MS. EVERTZ, HAS MY MOTHER BEEN SNOOPING AROUND MY OFFICE AGAIN?"

chapter 2

She's supposed to be the glue that keeps the family together, but the family business keeps getting in her way. She's confronted with the situations other moms can't even imagine, such as the time her husband and son had an argument at work and it carried over into the family's Thanksgiving dinner. Her role isn't defined by a title or a corner office, but, next to Dad, she probably has the most important job of all: peacekeeper. That's why we're calling her Mom, the Chief Family Officer.

If you're a mom reading this chapter, we'll explain the critical role you play in the family business. We'll show you how to keep the family together despite the fallout created at work. For other readers, you'll understand the benefit of having a Chief Family Officer and how an enlightened and empowered mom can diffuse conflicts, minimize bad feelings, and keep people talking. This chapter starts with a typical scenario of how business can affect family life, gives insights into Mom's issues, and offers her practical advice in the quest to keep the business from hurting her family.

Mom the CFO's Dilemma: A Typical Scenario

Is there a way to keep the business from hurting my family?

"It must be great to have your family working together in the business," my friend begins. "Your children live close by and you have a shared passion and purpose."

Maybe it used to be that way, but not anymore, I thought.

At the beginning, the business did seem to unite us. We were all rowing in the same direction and the business continued to grow. As the boys got older and married, things changed. My husband says they can't see eye-to-eye on anything–who should do what, where to spend the money, even the future of the business.

"Dad's not facing the changes in our industry," my son complains while calling to say he can't make it for dinner. "If we do everything his way, this business will go down the tubes." Disappointed at yet another cancelled family dinner, I confront my husband. "The business is ruining our family! We can't enjoy a simple dinner together anymore. Can't you do something?" My husband, as angry as my son, says, "Stay out of it! It's not your problem."

Oh, yeah? Then why can't I have dinner with my son tonight?

I'm tired of the office dominating my family's life. No matter what we do as a family, the business is the 800-pound gorilla in the room. If it's not the tension from a disagreement, than it's the inevitable shoptalk that breaks the group in two—the family members who work in the company and those who don't. The routine is aggravating: A nice chat in the kitchen turns into work when my husband asks my son, "Did you speak to the customer service rep on Friday?" Then they move to another room for the day leaving the rest of us to entertain ourselves. No one enjoys it and being together is beginning to feel more like an obligation. I even overheard my daughter-in-law say to my son, "Every time we're with your family it's always business, business, business. We need a break on the weekends!"

Her problem is, she's always sticking her nose where it doesn't belong and thinks she has the right to interfere. "My husband works harder than his brother, but gets no recognition," she told me. I wouldn't be surprised if she was encouraging him to go off on his own. Talk about starting World War III!

I've always stayed out of our family business. Maybe it's time to step in. But how? Who will listen to me? What can I do to keep the family from falling apart?

What's Mom Thinking?

An angry daughter, a fed-up son, an overwhelmed husband, a resentful in-law; that could be more painful for Mom than knowing her family doesn't enjoy being together anymore? Planning family events used to be a breeze. Now she needs a seating chart at dinner to separate people from each other. Family business Moms face an additional, powerful source of conflict that other moms don't–the business. When arguments at the office and unresolved bad feelings overshadow family time, Mom faces a seemingly impossible task–saving the family from the business-related problems.

Moms that have purposefully stayed away from the business are often shocked at the emotional fall-out from office disagreements. "How can my son refuse to speak to his sister?" she may think. "They've been best friends since they were children." Or, "My husband can't fire our niece! She's always been like a daughter to me." Constantly reacting to flare-ups that are out of her control, Mom may begin resenting the business and its imposition on her family. After all, she believes that blood is thicker than profit, and what happens at the office should stay at the office.

But it doesn't. And the consequences are too much to bear–family members are hardly on speaking terms, there is dinner table drama, and family function guest lists are dwindling. After all, how can Mom expect an invitation to her nephew's birthday celebration when he was just fired by her husband? Even when everything's rosy, the family and spouses may not want to get together after a long week at work. Isn't being together 40 or 50 hours a week enough without adding the weekends too?

In-laws often pose the biggest problems. A marriage may present a new, vocal player with his or her own interests and limited knowledge of past family history. For Mom, the universe of people affecting the family business expands, and she may feel everything was fine until a new spouse entered the picture.

In many cases, problems existed long before, but the family shoved them under the rug. Now, the conflicts are front and center. Is the new daughter-in-law egging her son on by suggesting he's treated unfairly, or is she rightly complaining that the old system of equal compensation for everyone is outdated and harmful to the business? Is the son-in-law wrong to encourage his wife to leave the family business, or is Dad's reluctance to put women in senior management holding her back?

Some Moms tell the in-laws to butt out. Others ignore the new spouse, hoping the country's 50-percent divorce rate will take care of the problem. Neither approach works. Angry confrontations create angry in-laws, while silence creates opportunistic ones.

If that isn't enough to cope with, Dad's retirement is yet another drama in which Mom stars as supporting actress. Some Moms want more time with their husbands, but they can't get him to let go of the business. Other Moms fear more time with their husbands because they've built a life of their own, and it doesn't include babysitting Dad all day. Add a sometimes-justifiable fear that retirement means a lot less income, and you have enough to rock even the most stable marriage.

So, how can Mom make things break her way? How can she keep the family peace in spite of the business conflicts? By embracing her unpaid title as Chief Family Officer and using her unique position to influence the outcome of events. In the next section, we'll show Mom the CFO exactly how to do that.

Five Action Steps for Mom the CFO

Action Step #1

Recognize that, next to Dad, you're the most influential person.

Mom, you may not have an official position, but trust us, you have enormous influence on the family business. Your power comes from two sources. First, you are the boss's wife, and no one in his or her right mind would insult, diminish, or ignore you. And, second, your position as the wife, mother, or mother-in-law commands respect in the family. So, don't sit on the sidelines. As Chief Family Officer, you can mix comforting words with principled power plays to break impasses, heal rifts, and improve work life. Think of yourself as operating out of a "virtual office." You bring it with you wherever you go. There are no e-mails or voice mails, but plenty of face time.

We don't want to you to weigh in on every family business decision or squabble. You may be the queen in your husband's kingdom, but wear the crown sparingly. Remember, influence is like a savings account: the more you use it, the less you've got. That said, Moms who ignore the business because they think it protects the family peace are out of touch with reality. We believe that separating the family from the business is impractical, and, in many cases, dangerous. As the Chief Family Officer, we think you have an important role to play and encourage you to A-C-T:

- **A**ccept the challenge of being a Mom in a family business. Know that conflicts are inevitable and that unconditional love isn't the top priority in business decisions. Also, know that you probably need to bite your tongue more than you'd like to with your in-laws. Your family life will be more intense than the family down the street, but that can be a good thing. Celebrate your family's status in the community and don't be afraid to blow your referee's whistle when the screaming match between your husband and your family spins out of control.
- **C**ultivate strong, meaningful relationships with everyone, including the in-laws. Find out what you have in common and keep in close contact. Showing genuine interest builds trust and provides access when problems develop. Does your son enjoy sports? Pick up some hard-to-find tickets and take him to a game he'll appreciate. Does your daughter like travel? Surprise her with reservations for a great, getaway weekend. Does your daughter-in-law love to cook? Go to a cooking class together. Get to know her parents by taking them to lunch periodically or making regular phone calls if they live out of town.
- **T**ake an interest in the business and be aware of issues and problems that could affect the family harmony. Being in-the-know is better than being out of touch. When you can say to your son, "I heard you had to take over your sister's department because she was having some problems," you have the credibility to continue a conversation

that may ease tension. On the other hand, saying, "I don't know anything about it and I don't want to know–I just want you to stop fighting with your sister," accomplishes nothing. Talk to your son about his anger toward his sister, but don't take sides. Listen to his complaints and then offer a different perspective that might lessen his resentment. Is sister unhappy with her career choice? Is she leaving the job earlier than her brother for legitimate reasons (such as picking up the children from daycare)? Is she distracted by her marriage or other personal problems? Whatever the answer, remind him that working in a family business is sometimes complicated. Share your own war stories, but with an emphasis on solutions.

An International Example

Mom Ends Family Feud in India

In 2005, India's stock markets rallied after news that the matriarch of family-controlled Reliance Group ended the fight between her two sons over who would control of the $23 billion company. The three-year dispute between the brothers ended when, due to Mom's intervention, the brothers agreed to split the company.

Action Step #2

Don't treat the in-laws like outlaws.

Win over your in-laws right away. Welcome them into the family in meaningful ways. Remember, marrying into an established family business is tough and scary even for the strong and brave. Make your in-laws feel included by being approachable and helpful, especially when they're curious about the family business. Sharing the past is like extending your hand and inviting someone into your home. When they want to know the skinny on why Uncle Bill isn't allowed to attend the Christmas party, who else better to tell the colorful story than you, the Chief Family Officer? By being warm and attentive, they'll understand the family and the business as much as you do.

Once your son or daughter marries, you can assume the family business is a regular topic of conversation at their house. Don't underestimate the influence this gives an in-law. They may not own stock or even work at the company, but trust us, they vote. While your son or daughter (or other family member) may work at the office from nine to five, your in-laws have their ear from five to midnight. When your son comes home frustrated with the family business, do you want your daughter-in-law preaching peace or fanning fights? Strong bonds with the in-laws can help you head off potential trouble.

The Big Point

Bite your tongue when you feel like telling your in-law, who's asking a lot of questions, to butt out of the family business. Remember, once they marry your child, they become de facto stakeholders in the business. The business affects their well-being as much as it does yours.

Is you son- or daughter-in-law working in the business? Please, be kind. Families often treat in-laws working in their business as second-class citizens. An unhealthy hierarchy can form in the office, especially if the in-law's resume is a little light. It isn't unusual for a family member to say something insensitive such as, "He can't fire you—he's Bob's brother-in-law."

Assume that any in-law working in the company isn't getting the respect the rest of the working family gets. Elevate their status by seeking them out socially. When the family sees that you have respect for the in-law, they will too. Remember, the boss's wife has the power to confer status. Besides, your in-law could one day run the business.

Action Step #3

Make family gatherings a work-free zone.

Think of yourself as a cruise director when you organize the family gatherings. The goal is a good time for everyone. And you do that by laying down the law: Homes are not an extension of the office. Set rules that make your family gatherings more family and less business. Here are five things to remember:

1. Limit shoptalk to 15 minutes. Tell your family you don't want the group separated into "those who work in the family business" and "others." Ban the office chatter at family events, but if that's impractical, at least try to control it. Use a timer and when it goes off in 15 minutes, feel free to interrupt the party poopers.
2. Yield the floor to family members who don't work in the business. Make everyone feel included and equally important. A simple question such as, "What's going on with you these days?" from someone in the family who works in the business to someone in the family who doesn't can change the tone of the whole evening. Ask about their career, recent travels, or feelings about local

politics. With the stay-at-home parent, discuss their volunteer work, involvement in sports, or the child's schools and activities.

3. Check the baggage at the door. Be playful but direct about keeping office issues out of the house. Put a bunch of airline baggage tags in a bowl outside your door and have everybody give you one as they come in. Tell them they can "claim their baggage" on their way out.
4. Choose fun, public places. Picking a neutral place heads off the natural tendency for families to compare their homes and exacerbate whatever office tensions exist. Public places greatly increase the chances of fun and relaxation because there's nothing there to remind them of office conflicts. They also provide distractions when there's tension in the group. Choose the new Mexican restaurant the grandkids will love, a Fourth of July parade and picnic, or a Sunday barbeque at the local park.
5. Be sensitive about frequency and locations. Understand that your in-laws may resent that all family get-togethers happen in your home, where they can't be totally relaxed. Rotate the location of holiday events as often as possible. Understand the group may not have the same degree of enthusiasm about spending nonworking time together as you do, so space events accordingly.

Action Step #4

Get outside help before the family assumes battle stations.

Don't wait until Armageddon to sound the alarm. If you wait until the point of no return you'll end up like we did–with the exits blocked and without experts who could help. In the end, one of the arbitrators we hired in a sibling dispute told us he had no way to put the genie back in the bottle. His words still echo in our ears: "Why didn't you call someone sooner?"

We delayed it for the same reasons every family resists hiring a family business consultant, a therapist, or arbitrator: It's embarrassing to admit the family is troubled, we didn't think it could help, and each person in the family thinks it's someone else's fault. So what happens? Nothing, and the problem gets worse.

How do you know when your situation warrants a third party's intervention? How do you get the help before it's too late? Start by making an objective assessment with our 10-question CFO test. You'll be the first to take it, and if you suspect there's enormous trouble brewing then have the main players in the family take the test too. The great thing about this test is, it doesn't place the blame on anyone. Use it as an altimeter to let you know if the family plane is flying a little too low and you need air traffic control's help.

The CFO Test

1. Do you sense a growing distance between you and family members (and their spouses) in the business?
2. Are you worried about your husband's health because he's under a different kind of stress than he's used to? Is he getting migraines when he never used to? Insomnia when he never had it?
3. Does just about every family gathering end in tension or disagreements?
4. Are there always last-minute no-shows to your family events?
5. Do some family members refuse to speak to each other?
6. Is office gossip about the family's relationship getting so pervasive that it's embarrassing?
7. Have customers made indirect statements or expressions on how the family soap is going?
8. Is Dad "skipping a generation" at family events and hanging out with his grandchildren because they're the only source of his pleasure?
9. Do you sense a connection between a loss of business and family strife?
10. Is Dad spending more time talking about trouble with the kids than the trouble with the business?

If you've answered yes more than you'd care to admit, it's time to swing into action. You really have only two options:

1. Gain consensus. Get members of the family to take the test. Their answers will most likely match yours. Your mission is to convince everyone that the family needs a third-party intervention. Always frame it in terms of "we," not "you." Avoid blame and emphasize optimism. It is possible to change business-busting family dynamics if you catch it early. Remind everyone, "We're all on the same train and if it doesn't change direction we're guaranteed to wreck!"
2. Pull rank. So, everyone takes the test, everyone agrees there's a problem, but nobody wants a third-party intervention. Now what? Find the best consultant/therapist/arbitrator, make an appointment, and make the meeting mandatory. Your secret weapon? Getting Dad on your side. And if you can't do it by appealing to reason then do it the old-fashioned way by making his life so miserable he'll give in just to get you off his back!

Action Step #5

Take an active role in Dad's retirement.

Dad probably has the entire family stressed out wondering when he'll let go, what he'll do, and how it will affect them. Do you want to do the family a big favor? Lead Dad into this new phase of life.

Translate, interpret, explain

Your first role is to be the bridge between Dad and the family when he needs an interpreter to convey what's behind his illogical moves and rhetoric. If he's similar to many family business Dads, he's uncomfortable with the R-word and doesn't care to discuss anything that reminds him of it. An innocent question such as, "Do you have any plans to take off a few weeks this summer?" generates suspicion. So, when you see your husband and others in the family talking across, above, and below each other, pull the kids aside and get to the real issues before they cause tension. Make sure each side understands what's really behind Dad's reactions.

We've given you a few classic misinterpretations that family members make of Dad's actions to see what we mean:

Dad's Action	What the Family Probably Thinks	What Mom Knows for a Fact
Suddenly involved in every decision.	He's an old bull that can't let go.	He's feeling irrelevant. He should be given the "chairman" title and a high-profile company project.
Won't officially turn over his "president" title.	His ego keeps getting in the way of succession.	He still wants to keep his power, his office, and his reserved parking space.
Won't discuss his financial situation and refuses to make succession plans.	He doesn't trust anyone in the company.	He's concerned about the nest egg, and would move aside if he had a way to secure it.

Map out his retirement plan

You have to be the diplomat, the interpreter, and now his retirement planner? What are we, crazy? Well, let's face it, *your* life may change as much as his when he retires. If you don't do something to manage him, he's going to end up managing you. Do you want to protect the life you've built for yourself? A life that doesn't include babysitting your husband seven days a week? Then, here's what you need to do:

- Look for the signs. You should be tuning in to what's going on at the office. For a fuller understanding of the transition process, read our "Father With Farewell Paranoia" chapter. You'll know the stage is set for the change when:
  1. Dad comes home earlier and grumpier because he feels left out of decisions.
  2. Family members give you hints that he needs to spend more time out of the office and pass the reins to the next generation.
  3. Dad's finding other interests and maybe talking about vacation homes.
- Help ease him out of the business. If you sense he's having difficulty with letting go, recruit friends and advisors to encourage him to take a first transitional step. Ultimately, you can start by suggesting a routine away from the office. If he can get away at 2 p.m. during the week, structure an activity to pique his interest and keep him busy. Are you able to take several weeks off in the summer? Spend them looking for a vacation residence where you can begin to plant roots.

- Help him find a purpose, some goals, and a lot of hobbies. If Dad already has a life outside of the business, congratulations! But many family business Dads are workaholics and haven't developed other interests–a sure sign that he's going to spend an inordinate amount of time berating the way you load the dishwasher. Don't let this happen. Take the initiative and determine what's best for both of you. Would Dad enjoy teaching what he's learned in the business? Check out the business program at the community college. Does he enjoy leading people? Volunteer organizations need management. Find one that interests him, such as the local children's shelter, Habitat for Humanity, or a civic organization. Many groups love tapping into business owners because they come with fat rolodexes, know how to make things happen, and have a knack for fundraising. Other Dads with an entrepreneurial spirit may want to start another business. Encourage him.

On the other hand, has he always wanted to be a great tennis player or golfer but never had the time? Look into local clubs that offer sports and social activities where he'll probably meet many people similar to himself. The main thing is to help him find a life, so he doesn't wreck yours!

Chapter Summary

Mom the CFO

Here's a summary of the five Action Steps you can take to keep the family business from disrupting the family harmony.

- ➡ **Action Step #1:** Recognize that, next to Dad, you're the most influential person in the family business. As Chief Family Officer, you have an important role to play. Take an interest in the business and be aware of the issues and problems that could affect the family.
- ➡ **Action Step #2:** Don't treat the in-laws like outlaws. You want them to embrace the family and the business as much as you do.
- ➡ **Action Step #3:** Make family gatherings a work-free zone.
- ➡ **Action Step #4:** Get outside help before the family looks like it's about to implode.
- ➡ **Action Step #5:** Do the whole family a favor and take an active role in Dad's retirement.

Chapter 3

The Hard-Charging Son

"Yes dad, I'll take an interest in the company - how does 50% sound?"

This Hard-Charging Son joined the family business with ambition and dreams of being in charge. He is fearless, sharp, and the most promising of Dad's kids. He is only missing experience–an unimportant footnote in his mind. Nevertheless, Son sees the company's potential, and is willing to bet Dad's bank to get there. Believing he's waited long enough, the Hard Charger is ready to get this party started and has big thoughts on how to reengineer the business. Who is standing in the way? Dad, of course! And Son knows if he pushes too hard, it could backfire and put his career on hold. He wants to be dealt in, but he's smart enough to know Dad holds all the cards.

If you're the Hard-Charging Son, this chapter will show you how to loosen Dad's stranglehold on the company without causing a tsunami at the office and in the family. You'll learn how to promote your ideas with Dad and get him to buy into your plan. We'll also give you a blueprint of how to win the respect of employees and family while broadening your own horizon with new thinking and mentors. For those wanting to understand the Hard-Charging Son, read on to see how he thinks and what the real issues are between him and Dad. Our typical scenario will illustrate the Hard-Charger's dilemma with insights on his behavior and recommendations to help him take over the family business with Dad's blessing.

The Hard-Charging Son's Dilemma: A Typical Scenario

How can I move dad aside without pushing too hard?

Something's gotta give. Dad has to start seeing things my way or I'm putting together my resume.

I've been here long enough and nothing's changed. I could write a novel faster than it takes to produce a simple financial report, and we still have the same people with last century's outlook. Fourteen months ago, I was so excited to leave my job and join the family business. I thought, "What a great opportunity to reshape the company and get us into the big time–open a new office, expand service lines, double revenue."

Now, I'm wondering why I came here. Yesterday I sat with Dad to go through my recommendations and get the company moving forward. It didn't go very well.

I opened the meeting with a sober assessment of the company. "Dad," I said, "Our resources are limited and a lot of our executives are still living in the past. We need to replace some of these old-timers and pump some new blood into the company. I've got some great ideas on how to get to the next level and–"

"Old-timers?" he yelled. "You're calling your uncle, your aunt, and my employees old-timers? The family that lent me money to meet payroll and employees that have stuck with me for years–are old-timers? If it wasn't for them, we might have gone bankrupt!"

Instead of the high-five I'd hoped for, I got a lecture on values: "Son, I reward loyalty; I don't punish it. When times were tough, they didn't jump ship. What if you spent 20 years helping your boss succeed and instead of showing appreciation he dumped you into the street?"

"By the way," he says diverting the conversation, "Who are the weird guys with the earrings I've seen you with lately?"

"They design Websites, Dad. We can reach a broader market by showing all of the services we offer. Besides, everyone has a Website," I suggest proudly.

"What?" he said. "Our customers could care less about that. They just want good service."

Another stall, but I saved the biggest recommendation for last. "Dad, I'd like you to see a presentation on the new software the competition is using. We'll need to make some changes to the management reports, but it will be worth it. We've got to get better and faster information."

"Forget about it," he said. "Joe tells me it always costs twice as much to get it up and running." Joe? His poker buddy from a company that's less than half our size? He's still listening to that caveman? Just then, the phone rang. Dad cupped the phone and said we'd talk later. Typical. Always putting me off when we're talking about my ideas.

I am so sick of this run-around. He shoots down every recommendation I have, no matter how good it is. There's no way this business will get to the next level without the changes I want to make. Why can't he see that? Dad's built a great business by anticipating and adapting, but now he's as flexible as concrete. I joined the family business because I wanted to learn from him and carry the torch into the next generation. But if he's so stuck in the past then what's the point of staying?

Maybe I should update that resume.

What's the Hard-Charging Son Thinking?

The Hard-Charging Son has his foot on the accelerator, while Dad has his foot on the brake. So, where are they going? Nowhere! The Hard Charger comes into the family business with an agenda: make it bigger, better, and install a new leader (him). Son's planning a revolution and can't understand why Dad doesn't want him to lead it. Sure, it requires some changes and more investment, but what about the benefits? What about the future? Son's passion, ambition, and feel for the newer, faster world of technology and globalization should be a breath of fresh air, but Dad's acting as though somebody cut off his oxygen supply. Why?

Son is missing a key ingredient in his approach–Dad's comfort zone. Driven by his own impatience, Son isn't taking Dad's concerns into account. In fact, he's as dismissive of Dad's concerns as Dad is of his. It's the old "which came first–the chicken or the egg" quandary between them. Is Dad dismissing Son because Son shows no concern for his issues? Or is Son indifferent to Dad's concerns because Dad won't listen?

Their endless loop revolves around four key issues:

1. **Business strategies:** Stay with the old or in with the new? Son is thinking new products, better service, state-of-the-art technology, and double-digit growth. Dad is thinking same products and service, same systems, reasonable growth.
2. **Employees:** Old guard or new blood? On the long-term employees, Son is thinking they're low on skills and high on salary. Dad is thinking they're high on loyalty and that's the price you pay for it.
3. **Advisors:** Major league or little league? Son is thinking Dad's advisors smell like mothballs. Dad's thinking they feel like a comfortable old shoe.
4. **Vendors:** Out to bid or out to lunch? Son is thinking that he should put everything out to competitive bid and let the price drive the selection. Dad is thinking don't fix what ain't broken.

So, Son wants to strap a rocket to the business and Dad wants to stay the course. Who's right? Both. Son's vision for the company's future is correct, but his disrespect of its past is not. He doesn't understand the art of diplomacy–getting more on Tuesday than what you gave up on Monday. Son needs to acknowledge his father's accomplishments, be an advocate for his top priorities, and then, S-L-O-W-L-Y advance his own ideas.

One of the reasons it is so hard for Dad and Son to see eye-to-eye is that they often relive their eye-for-an-eye relationship. Dad still remembers when Son wouldn't do as he was told and got them both in trouble. Such as the time when he warned him not to play ball in the neighbor's yard. Son ignored him and guess who had to pay for the neighbor's window? Then Son remembers all too well that Dad never seemed to appreciate his talents. He'd bring home report cards with a B+ average and all Dad could say was, "where are the As?"

The memories trigger old family software. Even a 6-foot-3-inch executive can turn into the little boy that Dad scolded at home. Worse, even a 60-year-old Dad, who never berates his employees in public, makes an exception for his son.

Can the Hard Charger and Dad avoid all the drama? After all, they both want the same thing–a successful family business; they just need to figure out how to get there. Consider this chapter a map on which the road to the hidden treasures of reconciliation, compromise, and shared vision are clearly marked. Yes, the land is pockmarked with lakes, rivers, and canyons, but it only takes a few steps to get to the other side.

Seven Action Steps to Get Dad to Move Aside

Action Step #1

Get tutored in Dad 101.

If you don't spend a little time getting a little insight into Dad's behavior or an appreciation for Dad's worries, you are never going to take over the business. The manual on understanding the family business father doesn't exist, but the next best thing does–Mom. Get her advice, but don't raise her blood pressure by announcing you've had it with the company. Instead say, "Mom, I'm trying to help Dad move the company forward, but I sense he's resisting. Do you have any advice for me?"

If she's read our Mom chapter and embraces her Chief Family Officer role, Mom should be able to tell you what Dad's thinking. (Reading Chapter 1 can help you, too). Is he afraid your changes will disrupt the entire company and distract managers from their jobs? Does he think your ideas are great, but you're acting like a bull in a china shop? Once you have her insight, ask how she would approach him. Is he too distracted at the office? Would it be better to talk at home or the office? At night or during the day? A quick Saturday morning breakfast? Or a leisurely weekday lunch? If you're still having a difficult time getting a read on Dad, consult with other family members that may help.

The Big Point

Put Dad's Shoes On

How does giving you more authority affect him? Will he lose status? Get pushed out of the information flow? Because he's probably too embarrassed to discuss such small and petty things openly, ease his mind. Give him something concrete to show you're addressing his concerns–schedule weekly update meetings and status reports, copy him on e-mails, include him on conference calls.

Action Step #2

A second start might be smart.

Once Mom or other family members help you understand Dad's worries and concerns, ask Dad for a meeting. Here's how we want you to phrase it: "Dad, I've been doing a lot of thinking, and I can see many of your business points. Can we sit down and talk about how I can contribute more to the company?" This conciliatory gesture will neutralize his defensiveness, increase his willingness to talk about a subject that's always ended in disaster, and make him more receptive to what you want.

Do *not* go into this meeting cold. You'd never wing a meeting with a client that could double your business, so be prepared.

Before the meeting:

- **Remember with whom you're talking.** Dad got where he is without you.
- **Practice calmness.** That means keeping your trap shut and your jets cooled when he says something you think is unfair or dismissive, because he most likely will. The best way to regulate your emotions is to practice saying phrases such as, "I'd feel the same way if I were you," or, "I understand why you feel that way." Another way to instill calm into the conversation is to watch your language. Don't call his long-term employees "old-timers," his strategy "outdated," or his advisors "brain-dead." They are disrespectful phrases and add nothing to the conversation except conflict.

- **Get clear on your purpose.** You're not meeting to unload all your anger and resentment. You're meeting to ask Dad how you can better help the company. Turn "me" into "we" and you'll find him far more receptive.

At the beginning of the meeting:

- **Take responsibility.** Yes, he's caused you a lot of grief, too, but he's not going to be the first to apologize or acknowledge he owns half of the mess between you. By doing it first, you're showing the maturity he probably thinks you lack. So start off by saying something such as, "You know what, Dad? I made a mistake. In my rush to help the business grow, I've been impatient and not as respectful of your feelings or accomplishments as I should have been. I think it would be hard for anybody to weigh my recommendations on their merits without first reacting to my negative approach. So I'd like to wipe the slate clean and start the conversation about my role in the company from scratch."
- **Thank him.** Not for the meeting but for everything he's done–for you, your family, even the community. Tell Dad why you joined him in the first place. Tell him what you've learned from him and how much you admire what he's accomplished. Be specific. Be sincere.
- **Go over the company's strengths.** Tell him who and what impresses you. Is it the superior service? A strong customer base? An established brand? A dependable staff? Be sure you have specific examples.

In the middle of the meeting:

- **Bring up your ideas as possibilities, not inevitabilities.** First, explain how your ideas will make the company better. Acknowledge that Dad has a right to be skeptical and that you're asking for consideration, not implementation. For example, you want to build a full-blown Website that he thinks is a waste of time. Suggest a market survey of your existing and potential customers to gauge its usefulness. Show him competitor's Websites and give him a range of costs for different levels of programming. Ask him if he'd be willing to attend a presentation or two. *Demand* and his answer will be no; ask and his answer may be yes.

At the end of the meeting:

- **Ask direct questions.** Ask Dad if he thinks you're ready for more responsibility. If the answer is yes, settle on your new projects or areas you can supervise and tell him you'll make him proud. Most importantly, bring up concrete timetables and evaluation criteria before he does. You'll gain his respect and possibly his help.

If Dad is less confident, go back to asking. For example, you can ask, "What projects can I do for you that will give you more confidence in me?" Remember, he doesn't want you to fail, but at the same time, he doesn't want to put the business at risk, either. So suggest a plan that will showcase your skills, increase your visibility, along with a timetable so you can show him your progress. After a few successfully completed projects, you should have earned your wings.

What should you do if Dad doesn't budge? You really only have two choices. If you're still relatively new to the business and believe he'll come around in time, recalibrate your level of intensity. Make sure there are set benchmarks to assess your performance and that he knows when you've met them. If there are not formal performance reviews in the company, sit down with Dad at appropriate intervals (every six to eight months) and discuss your progress.

On the other hand, if you've met the benchmarks and see that Dad just wants you to be his gopher until he retires, you need to rethink your immediate future in the family business. Can you live with it? Or would you be better off polishing up your skills elsewhere? If you're ready to pack your bags, relay your decision in a nonthreatening way. Say to Dad, "I love and respect you, but it feels like there's no place for me here now. I'd like to move on to another company, sharpen my skills, and hopefully join you in a few years." If he agrees, then clear out your office. If he doesn't, negotiate a final four-month "extension plan." If you meet his benchmarks, you advance; if you don't then you have the choice of staying until you do, or leaving with the possibility of coming back.

One final note: Don't expect Dad to take his hands off the wheel until he feels you can drive. When you get to the point that you can race through the industry's obstacle course without knocking down any of the orange cones, he'll hand you the keys to the kingdom.

The Big Point

Complete, Don't Compete

Don't tell Dad his ways are outdated or that new blood could grow the business faster than his Old Guard. He's looking for an heir that'll complete him not compete with him. Treat him as a mentor–you'll learn more and rise faster.

An International Example

The Hard-Charging Son in Malaysia

Francis Yeoh, a true hard-charging son, took over YTL Corp. At age 24, he credits Dad with having the humility to give him the reins to a modest construction company that he built into an international business empire.

Action Step #3

Become the go-to guy at the office.

The best way to move your agenda forward is to become an acknowledged leader at the company. We understand you are impatient, but leadership isn't awarded, it's earned. You aren't going to walk through the company doors and be crowned "boss" overnight. In fact, you'll need to be more convincing because you are family. Just having ideas you've gleaned from reading *Business Week* or sitting in a college classroom isn't enough. You have to deliver. Here's how:

Get fit

Get your area or department in top shape. Create a following of believers who praise you behind your back, or, at the very least, respect you. Once you've had some successes, become visible in other parts of the company. Walk around, kick the tires, say hello. Figure out ways to make employees appreciate working for the company, but especially for you. It could be as simple as buying a new coffee machine or comfy chairs for the lounge, sponsoring a weekly Chinese lunch delivery, or surprising them with ice cream on a hot summer afternoon. Don't just care; express that caring in meaningful ways. Encourage people to talk to you, but never respond negatively or raise your voice with others around. Query the group—how can we make things better? What's on their wish list?

Become the leader you want as a boss

Ambitious and smart? Sure, that's important, but you'd better manage people well if your goal is convincing Dad to move aside. Show him you're a leader and you can pull together a variety of people in the company to solve problems. Suggest projects that affect the entire company so Dad sees you working across departments. Once you've gotten his okay, pick your team. If current management doesn't have any fresh ideas and you can't hire someone, consider bringing in a temporary project consultant who is more up-to-date. Be sure to include some of the regulars in the company. Take over the conference room to formalize your leadership position, and hold regular staff meetings that eventually become the place where all the news is disseminated. Reward individual contributions publicly by handing out merit checks or other rewards for work well done. Thank people.

As an example, let's say your first project is to reduce the company's debt level and you believe better cash management will do the trick. Your staff suggests sending invoices earlier and shortening the time between collection calls. They recommend payments be scheduled to take advantage of discounts or newly negotiated terms. If their suggestions hit the mark, reward their efforts with a cash reward and public recognition.

What are some other ways to reinforce your go-to guy image? Scan the horizon for better products and faster service; sign up for industry trade shows and take key staffers to see the new approaches; bring in vendors to demonstrate their latest offerings; be the link to the outside world.

Employees love bosses who invest in them, so make training a priority and part of every employee's career plan. As you consider the areas in which you want to improve in the company, keep up with the latest books on leadership, team-building, and management for new ideas. Discuss your thoughts with a mentor and others outside of the family business to get a different perspective.

Action Step #4

Fix problems without getting yourself into a fix.

As you develop thoughts on improving the company, keep in mind Dad's biggest concern: You're going to create a bigger mess than you'll solve because you won't know the ramifications of your changes. He'll think your youth and inexperience will blind you to not-so-obvious pitfalls. If you want Dad to move in your direction, show him how you've anticipated his concerns. Earlier, we talked about the most common areas of Dad-Son conflicts: how to manage business strategies, employees, high-level advisors, and vendors. Let's review them, case by case, and see how each party views the subject and how you can reconcile the differences.

The case: Business strategies

Background: Sales are slowing, expenses are growing. The conference room was last used in the first Bush presidency and it's practically covered with cobwebs.

Dad: "I've gone through these down cycles before. I have a proven track record. I know what works and what doesn't. The business will bounce back–it always has before.

Son: "It's a different world. What worked in the past won't work tomorrow. We need new products, better service, and bleeding-edge technology."

The Verdict: Okay, you're both right. Maybe some things are outdated, but you can't flip a switch and install the new plan overnight. Opening a new office, installing new software, and replacing the sales manager can't be done in your first month. Dad knows turmoil and disruption is the last thing a family business needs. After all, if the business is typical, the company's stability is one of its greatest assets. Dad wants to hear how you will enhance the company, not dismantle it.

Dad will be more open to your suggestions if he believes you understand the company's strengths. Review the principles that made the company successful. Are they still working, but need some updating? Example: Dad built the business by being the low-cost provider. In the last two years, expenses have been creeping up, lowering margins, and making it difficult to price your service competitively. Can you turn it around with some nips and tucks instead of major surgery? We recommend starting smaller. For a nip and tuck, talk Dad into testing your suppliers' prices through a competitive bidding process. What's major surgery? Outsourcing the entire administrative department. We're not saying it's not a good idea, but put a few feathers in your cap before you pluck the whole bird.

The case: Employees

Background: Hired years ago, the long-term employees perform the job exactly as they always have. Solid? Yes. Stellar? No.

Dad: "How do you put a price on loyalty? I'd rather pay higher-than-average salaries and keep turnover low. Do you know what it costs to train new people?"

Son: "Merit and CPI increases brought their salaries way beyond market levels. We're basically paying them with money we don't have for skills they don't have."

The Verdict: Purging Dad's long-term employees may be more dangerous than you think. They come with intimate knowledge of the company, a nd developed relationships with customers, vendors, and employees. At first glance, you may think that the way someone does something is ridiculously outdated or unnecessary. But don't fall into the trap of making fast judgments. First, you have to play detective and find out who does what, who knows what, and how much they're paid (relative to what they do).

If you find the staff is lacking in skills, it may be because Dad never instituted a formal training program. If so, give them a chance to prove themselves. Invest in a training period (say three months), then check on their progress. Determine if investing further will get them closer to the benchmark. If it's not working, you'll have the basis to make changes and prove to Dad you've made a considered decision. Hopefully, training combined with a renewed focus on performance will do the trick. It will cost the company much less to keep the existing crew than hiring a new group that may not stay with the company.

Long-term, high-level managers with yesterday's skills are trickier. They are usually an institution at the company and a big part of its culture. Training probably won't solve your problems, but throwing them out in the street will create havoc. Even if rank-and-file employees agree with your assessment, treating the manager disrespectfully will leave employees angry and feeling threatened. Better to a pay a few extra dollars to keep the employee on (if possible) and hire a replacement that will eventually take over the responsibilities. Plan for a transition to last at least 4 to 6 months; be as generous as possible with severance; or better still, consider using the manager as a special project consultant.

What can you do if you are satisfied with an employee, but their compensation package is out of line? You and the employee have to pick one of two options: either increase their responsibilities or decrease their salary. In your meeting with the employees, be prepared with documentation showing their job's market value and the value of jobs with more responsibilities. Encourage them to stay, emphasize your plans for their careers, but understand they might not like either option and decide to leave.

The case: Advisors

Background: Dad uses the same one-stop shop for all his legal, accounting, and tax services that he used 15 years ago. Dad is their biggest client and he refuses to switch. Most of his other advisors are family friends from way back.

Dad: "Why should I fix something that isn't broken? They've done right by me. Besides, I'd rather be a big fish in a small pond. If I go somewhere else, they'll treat me like a number and I'll get lost in the cracks.

Son: "His advisors don't have the expertise we need or the guts to call him out when he's wrong. Worse, I'm not sure they even know when he's wrong. We need a big-league law firm and an accounting firm that can advise us on technology and tax strategies."

The Verdict: Tread carefully. If you think changing Dad's long-term employees is going to be tough, wait'll you try to touch these guys. Our advice: Add, don't subtract. Hire new firms for new projects, but have Dad's advisors review their work. Teaming seasoned veterans with young Turks doesn't cut out anybody. Dad will have the comfort of old friends and you'll have the satisfaction of introducing new ideas. Eventually, the older advisors will float away without you incurring Dad's wrath. In the meantime, the company gets the best of both worlds.

The case: Vendors

Background: Through the years Dad's vendors have morphed from service providers to "friends." He's never challenged the yearly price increases or recent shipping surcharges.

Dad: "I trust these guys. Yeah, they're more expensive, but they give me the intangibles–shortcuts and little known industry secrets that have helped my bottom line for years."

Son: "I know we can save a ton of money by stopping no-bid contracts and pit vendors against each other. Maybe we can get better payment terms. We could use the savings to fund our expansion."

The Verdict: This should be the easiest area to reconcile because the results are so quantifiable. Start by testing bids with vendors that don't have their hooks in Dad so deeply. You'll convince Dad about the merits of bidding if it fattens up the bottom line. You may even get the best of both worlds–Dad's preferred vendor at the lowest price.

The Big Point

Avoid The KSB Syndrome

New leaders, especially men, have a tendency to think the best way to prove themselves is to *Kill Something Big*–as in firing a senior officer of the company. Avoid the "I'm in charge here" ego swagger. Instill respect, not fear.

Action Step #5

Become the diplomat in the family.

Instead of the "Hard Charger," do others in the family see you as the "Hard Pusher"–always looking out for yourself at everyone else's expense? Or worse, are you considered the "renegade"–off in your own world with little regard for the family who might not like you? If you've answered yes, you've got to change your stripes if you want Dad on your side.

Become the diplomat, the one who can bring the family together, and you'll show Dad he'll be appointing a good steward of his legacy.

The office is not the place to try upstaging relatives. When your sister makes an error with a customer, complaining behind her back doesn't help you or the family. Employees may join in the bashing, but they'll be uncomfortable when it's over. Instead, be as supportive and helpful as possible. Here are some of the most common issues you'll face and how you can neutralize them:

Issue	What Not to Do	What to Do
Sister publicly speaks poorly of other family members.	Join in with her and turn up the heat.	Take her aside and describe how it marginalizes her and doesn't unify the family.
Father and brother are in a heated exchange over a business issue.	Hold their coats while you watch the fight.	Hear them out individually, bring them together and broker a peace.
Brother is struggling in the business.	Point it out to everyone.	Lend a helping hand and keep the critique to yourself.
Niece's divorce is affecting her job performance.	Keep reminding her why her husband left.	Treat her warmly and offer to temporarily adjust her schedule.

Action Step #6

Let an outsider in.

Alexander the Great had Aristotle. Nixon had Kissinger. Even the Godfather had his consigliore. Unless your father is Bill Gates or Jack Welch, you probably could use advice from a successful outsider who's been there, done that.

What's the biggest advantage in having a mentor? Warding off the tunnel vision so common in family businesses. Ideally, your mentor should run a company larger than yours and be well established in the business community. Here are some other things your mentor can do to make life easier for you:

- Share in their experiences as you encounter the typical business growing pains.
- Provide contacts and open doors to highly regarded firms and potential customers.
- Give you advice on handling family influences in the business.
- Raise your visibility in the business community through membership in charitable or civic organizations and clubs.

So, how do you find Mr. or Ms. Mentor to make your life easier? First, resist the temptation to stay in the family, even if your aunt, who is neutral on Dad, has a wildly successful business. Why? Your mentor should be close enough to understand what you're going through, and far enough to provide objective advice. If you have a network through a previous job or school contacts, start there and let them know what you're looking to accomplish.

When there's no obvious candidate, begin your search at the local chamber of commerce or a high-profile charitable or civic group that attracts influential, successful people.

The Big Point

Movers and shakers don't have lunchboxes. They're too busy attending lunchtime meetings at their favorite charitable or civic organization. If you're on the hunt for your mentor, join a high-profile organization and volunteer your time on a committee.

Don't be shy about chatting up someone you admire and asking their advice. Everyone's flattered to be asked their opinion. If you're lucky enough to have a local college or university with a family business or entrepreneurial program, check out their Website. Many programs offer mentoring matches and services.

Your best bet to move the family business forward with ideas and professionalism is to establish an outside advisory group or a board of directors. This group looks at the business from a different vantage point and can offer the outsider's perspective you may sorely need. Similar to your mentor, they can also open doors and provide contacts. Most important, councils and boards encourage the family to feel accountable to the business rather than just the family.

If Dad hasn't formed such a group yet, it's probably because he doesn't feel comfortable revealing revenue, profitability, or compensation information to outsiders. After all, they may call him on deteriorating business performance or his excessive compensation package, or question why his sister has a high-paying, no-show job. You may have to convince him that for the company's good, you need to take this step. Start with an advisory group and tell Dad you'll save money on the director's and officer's insurance required with a formal board. Select one or two independent people–they don't have any business with or receive any compensation from the company. Try to have a meeting three to four times per year.

The Big Point

Don't Let Family Ties Put You in a Bind

Your business should have an outside advisory board, period. After you get to a certain size, it's vital to the success of your company. If difficult family relationships stop you from forming one, it's time to call a family business consultant and broker a peace, so the company gets the benefit of a new perspective.

Action Step #7

Promote Dad to the top job.

So you've met his benchmarks, successfully changed some of the business strategies and operations, saved a bundle by making vendors compete, installed new advisors, became the family diplomat, earned the respect of your staff, and Dad still hasn't stepped aside. Why? Because you skipped the final class in Dad-ology. The one that teaches you how to make him think you're putting him up on a pedestal, not out to pasture. Here's the one and only lesson: Make Dad feel needed. Make him an integral part of the business. Do it by saying, "Dad, I can't do this without you. I need your expertise. What if we bumped you up to chairman and me to CEO?"

Convince him that this isn't a move out the door, but up the ladder. Convince yourself, too, because we're not recommending this as a PR move. Statistics show that when Dad stays on as a senior advisor, family businesses have a much greater likelihood of success. So, this isn't about sparing Dad's feelings; it's about securing the future of the company. Dad's presence, in his new role, gives your employees and customers a sense of security and continuity. He's the greatest asset the company has, so use him wisely.

How do you convince Dad that the time is right? Here are some recommendations:

- First, discuss your readiness with him. List your successes and tell him your plans to make the family business a legacy of which he'll be proud.
- Emphasize the affect you'll make within and outside the company once you are president.
- Stress the relevance of this step to his plan to pass the baton to a family member.
- Be ready to discuss how this will affect his day-to-day routine.

He'll be curious about your plans for him, so be armed with plenty of ways to leverage his power, such as special projects, customer service or "high-touch" events, community outreach, and participation in the local political scene. As for salary and perks, it's best to leave them unchanged for now (unless it puts financial pressure on the company), and let him get used to his new role.

The Big Point

Have a Two-way "Gentleman's Understanding"

Dad can attend any meeting and ask any questions, but he must always voice concerns to Son privately. In return, Son should never make a major financial commitment without consulting Dad.

Chapter Summary

The Hard-Charging Son

Here's a summary of the seven Action Steps to show Dad he can move aside and give you more responsibility in the family business. Take these steps and you'll convince him you can be trusted with the keys to the kingdom.

- **Action Step #1:** Understand Dad and his concerns about changing business strategies, employees, advisors, and vendors. Let Mom or someone else close to him fill in the critical missing pieces as you put yourself in his shoes.
- **Action Step #2:** Meet with Dad and discuss how you can contribute to the company. Make Dad feel that you are there to complete him, not compete with him.
- **Action Step #3:** Establish your leadership credentials by becoming the go-to guy at the office.
- **Action Step #4:** Tackle small problems first. You'll earn Dad's trust and respect with your successes. Remember, the worst thing you can do is over promise and under deliver.
- **Action Step #5:** Become the diplomat in the family. You'll show Dad you are the perfect steward for the family business.
- **Action Step #6:** Find a mentor outside of the business. Establish an advisory group or board of directors, if Dad hasn't already.

➡ **Action Step #7:** Recognize that Dad is an asset to the family business. Keep him around as chairman when you take the president title to preserve continuity for employees and customers.

In-Laws Under the Influence

"Home, job, wife ... I've lost everything."

Has your spouse's family business become the center of the universe, it's influence spilling over into every part of your life? If so, we've dedicated this chapter to you. Forgetting gender for the sake of clarity, we're placing you into two main categories and dividing the chapter into two parts with separate scenarios, insights, and recommendations.

chapter 4

- **Part 1: The Son-in-Law.** You're either thinking about joining your wife's family business or you work in it now. You're wondering what you should consider before joining the business and how to protect yourself once you're there.
- **Part 2: The Supportive Spouse.** You don't work in your in-law's business, but your hubby does. You want him to be treated fairly and can't find the logic in many of the business decisions that affect your household.

No matter which kind of in-law you are, we know you sometimes feel as though you are playing pavement to the family business steamroller, struggling to figure out where you fit in and how you can have a say in what goes on. Whoever you are, we're going to help you find your voice, give you some insight, and recommend ways of keeping peace in your marriage while recognizing your role in the family business.

Part 1: The Son-in-Law Dilemma: A Typical Scenario

What should I consider before joining my spouse's family business and how do I protect myself once I join?

Should I join my wife's family business? Before I do, I'm meeting with an old friend who has worked for his wife's family business since we graduated.

I see him at the table, on his cell, waving his hand at me. "Yes, sir, they'll be at the trade show tomorrow. Yes, the hotel is aware. I've taken care of it," he says. Afterward, he rolls his eyes, apologizing again.

"Hey," I begin, "You're leaving for a trade show tomorrow? Your customers sound a little frantic. We could have rescheduled."

"I'm not going to the trade show," he starts, "but my wife's father and brother are. Those weren't customers. It was my father-in-law doing his 'did ya, did ya' routine."

We finally get around to my big question–what is it like to work in your wife's family business? He turns off the cell and gives me a sigh before he starts.

"After we graduated, I was offered a position in administration. It's not what I wanted, but the money was great. I spend my day in drudgery while the stars of business are in sales and production."

"Can't you talk to someone?" I suggested. "After all, you're family in a family business."

"Family? That's not the way it works. My goose was cooked the day I told my father-in-law his bickering with his son should be behind closed doors because every employee could hear it. I thought he was going to strangle me. 'Who do you think you are?' he screamed. My wife even knew about it when I got home. I just keep my nose to the grindstone now. My advice to you–think long and hard about it before you make a move!"

Great, I thought. What a ringing endorsement. All I'd been thinking about was the high pay, the perks, and fast-track promotions. I mean, I *am* married to the boss's daughter, but my friend just turned my vision of heaven into hell. Now what do I do?

What's the Son-in-Law Thinking?

Decisions, decisions, decisions. You'll rarely make a more important one than joining the family business. It's easy to see why you shouldn't–many people think being with their in-laws twice a year during holidays is two times too much; they can't even imagine working for them. Not without a standing reservation at the mental health clinic.

What's not so easy to see is why you *should* work for them: financial security, fast-track promotions, and a boon to your children's future. All, of course, if everything works out and everyone gets along. A big *if,* but an *if* worth exploring. Most in-laws contemplating the leap draw up a mental list of pros and cons. We suggest you put it on paper, start with these issues, and fill in your own:

Pros	Cons
You don't feel secure with your job. The family business promises security.	You'll get all the security you want—as long as your marriage stays intact.
The business has problems that your skills and experience could solve.	Family politics and jealousies often make it hard to do the job you were hired for.
Your spouse receives stock in the business. You could add value by contributing your expertise to the company.	The chances of you getting any stock personally may be slim, so you'll have to stay married.
If business is booming and they need all hands on deck, this could be your chance to ditch that job you hate or switch industries.	If you get divorced, this benefit could change.
Working for the family might be an easier ride than the job you have.	You'll get the "freeloader" label quickly if you don't pull your own weight.

As you can see, much of your decision rests on the state of your relationship with your spouse. For the sake of everyone's sanity, don't even *think* about joining the family business if you've got a rocky marriage.

Even if you've got a solid marriage, joining the family business doesn't come with guarantees. Intra-family power plays, manipulation, and second-class citizenship can leave you feeling like a pawn in someone else's chess game. Unless you're willing to deal with incompetent family members, long-term employees who shouldn't be there, and the kind of sibling rivalries that make peace in the Middle East seem like an attainable goal, you are not going to be a happy person.

Many in-laws are afraid to ask the tough questions before they join the business; for example, asking about succession plans may seem too personal, too uncomfortable. But what happens when Dad's long-lost brother steps into the top job? Too late. You should have asked about it before you joined. Some in-laws naturally *assume* they'll get stock in the business after a few years, so they never ask. What if you don't? Too late. You can't complain about something you never asked about.

Let's be clear–if you're not tough enough to ask some of the questions we recommend, you won't be tough enough to be successful in the business. Asking the right questions upfront lays the groundwork for a more predictable experience once you've joined.

When you work for the family business, you never know whether the fins swimming around you belong to friendly dolphins or angry sharks. Whether you're thinking about taking the plunge or wondering how to stay afloat without getting devoured, we've got plenty of lifesavers to throw at you.

Two Action Steps for the Son-in-Law

Action Step #1

Don't join unless you're invited.

Working for your father could lead to justifiable homicide, but working for your spouse's father? Suicide. We believe it's such a dicey proposition, you shouldn't even consider it unless they've rolled out the red carpet and offered you a very attractive package. If the family didn't pursue you, you'll have about as much influence as the janitor. Actually, he'll have more because they *need* him. Both of you will wear uniforms to work, only yours better be made of thick skin.

However, if the family is pursuing you it means they see enormous value in you despite the fact that you're an in-law. Read the fine print on the in-law label–it's considered recyclable by many families. But again, if the family's courting you, we think you should definitely consider it.

But let's not get ahead of ourselves. Your first stop on the way to making a decision is your spouse's favorite restaurant. The two of you have a lot to discuss. After all, this job affects your spouse as much as it does you. How does your spouse get along with his or her parents and siblings? Does he or she think working for the family is a good idea?

What kind of relationship does your spouse currently have with the rest of the family? Is your wife still daddy's little girl? Does she feel he can do no wrong, that he's bigger than life? If so, think about the consequences of tangling with him in the office. Is your husband ferociously protective of his younger brother? If so, what happens if you end up working and disagreeing with him?

Those are the good examples. What if your spouse *doesn't* get along with the family? If that's the case, here's our advice: run, don't walk. Even if she wants to grow closer to them you'll end up being the crash-test dummy in an endless family car pile-up.

Let's say all the stars line up—the family pursues you, your spouse has a great relationship with the family, and they've offered an attractive package. Should you take it? Not so fast. Not until you answer this critical question: What happens to my job if my marriage fails? The answer: What job? We don't care how valuable you are to the company, your job ends the day your marriage does. There are some exceptions, but not many. Who betrayed who could be the deciding factor in your favor. Here are a few scenarios:

Grounds for Divorce	What Happens to You
You decide to marry a woman you met at the office.	Both of you should pack your bags. If you don't have a severance agreement, you won't get a dime from Dad.
Your wife just doesn't love you anymore.	50/50 chance of keeping your job. If you're a very productive guy, odds are better.
You just don't love your wife anymore.	You're toast. You'll be lucky to get out with your reputation in tact.
Your wife leaves you for a woman.	Best-case scenario: You might even make it to retirement.

An International Example

Wanted: Son-in-Law in South Korea

This Dad is so desperate for a son-in-law to marry his 38-year-old daughter and carry on the family business that he placed an ad in an Internet match-making agency. The millionaire Dad received 200 applications in four days even though he described his daughter as follows: "Despite the shortcomings of being a bit too old and short, she is top-notch in terms of other conditions."

Action Step #2

Get the issues on the table before you get on the payroll.

Before you graciously accept an offer, schedule a serious, and frankly, uncomfortable conversation with whoever is making the offer (father, mother, uncle, brother, sister). Here's the procedure we recommend:

- **Location, Location, Location.** Pick one that's comfortable, not confrontational. A private room in a restaurant works. A lawyer's office doesn't.
- **Preparation, Preparation, Preparation.** Get every detail about the family from your spouse, so you know who does what, where, and how. Then talk to a lawyer who is not affiliated with the family or the business, preferably a specialist in family business. Have him advise you on legal questions before your meeting.
- **Throw the softballs first.** Because many of your questions will raise everyone's blood pressure, start out on a congenial note. For example, tell

your father-in-law that you've discussed the offer with your wife/his daughter and that she's fully supportive. He probably already knows this, but reinforcing his daughter's happiness never hurts. Go over the perfunctory questions you would ask any potential employer: Who do you report to? How will your performance be reviewed? Will you be groomed to take over positions above you?

➡ Throw the hardballs next. Go through scenarios that don't exist at any other employer:

1. Do the other family members think it's a good idea for you to join the business? He'll never name names, but you can ask if there are dissenting opinions about you working there. If he says, yes it doesn't bode well for you. If he says everyone's on board, you're golden.
2. Does he have a succession plan? If not, what are his ideas? Best to know upfront if you have a shot at it, or worst, if an in-law you don't like is being groomed for the big job.
3. Will you be given stock in the company? Some family businesses give stock to in-laws; others don't. If you're discussing a high-level job, this is a perfectly legitimate question.
4. What happens if you get divorced? First, he'll stammer, then he'll bob and weave. Don't press too hard because he'll never come out and tell you the truth. Still, it's worth asking, because it shows that you're thinking ahead and projecting worst-case scenarios—business skills he'll appreciate.
5. Does he have any plans to sell the business? Would he consider selling it to you under the right circumstances?

6. Will you be eligible for the same perks as other family in the business? This includes profit distribution, expense accounts, company cars, and other benefits.

What if you don't get the answer you're looking for? Thank him for the opportunity. Tell him you're seriously considering the offer and would like to talk again, if necessary. Remember, you may have caught him off guard with some questions, so leave the meeting graciously and have a bunch of powwows with your wife and lawyer to determine the next step.

The Big Point

Severance Agreement, Please

Remember, you'll be subject to more emotional decision-making in a family business than in nonfamily businesses. Will your wife's dad fire you for looking at the new sales woman the wrong way? Don't chance it. Protect yourself with a severance agreement.

If your answer is no...

...you'll have to bow out gracefully without insulting everyone. Here's an example of the tone to use with your two biggest constituents: Dad and Wife.

To Dad, say something such as, "I am so honored to feel included in the family. Considering me for a position in the family business is a big compliment that has caused me enormous conflict. I wish I could go with my heart and join immediately. But, I'm afraid to risk my relationship with you and the rest of the family. Many times mixing family and business just doesn't work out. I do this out of love and respect." Hopefully, he'll understand and you'll have the same relationship in the future as you did before the job offer.

To your wife, say something like, "Your Dad has been extremely generous, but our marriage is the most important thing in my life, and I don't want to put any pressure on it by joining the family business. Maybe it's something to consider in the future." She should be pleased that you are so concerned about your marriage.

If your answer is yes...

...welcome, and let the games begin! The most important one is keeping that target off your back and staying out of the family's shooting range. Here are some of the most common challenges you'll face and how to deal with them.

Problem: Spouse turns nightly conversation into a Q&A to get the low-down on the family.

Solution: Set stringent rules regarding who you'll talk about and for how long you'll talk. Your spouse has a right to know what's going on, but you have a right to leave the job at the office. Find a middle ground; 20 minutes of office gossip sounds about right, so does framing everything in the most positive light. We don't recommend telling your wife that her dearest brother botched the client meeting by bringing another client's PowerPoint presentation. Some things are better left unsaid.

Problem: Spouse's siblings get better perks than you do.

Solution: Swallow your pride. If you didn't have the foresight to ask about this upfront, you don't really have the right to complain about it. Besides, the real issue is whether your perks are in line with *your* job, not the sibling's. If you've got similar jobs at similar levels, you've got three options: (1) Take it up with Dad. Not that it'll do much good. He'll most likely say, "It's none of your business how I take care of my family;" (2) leave. We think that's rather harsh. There are better reasons to make an exit. Wait for them; they're probably right around the corner; (3) forget about it. We heartily recommend this option. Unfair disparities between family and in-law perks come with the territory. As long as your compensation and benefits track with market averages, we say leave the issue alone. You don't need to wonder if another family member is getting more perks. They are.

Problem: You're being pressured to take sides in spouse's family.

Solution: STAY AWAY. Stick to the talking point that always worked for us: "Look, I promised my spouse I wouldn't do anything to jeopardize our family relationship, and you're asking me to do that." That kind of honesty should win you a get out of jail free card. On the other hand, if you feel compelled to take a side for business or family reasons, first, discuss it with your spouse, because it affects his or her relationship with family. Be sure to explain it so there's no doubt you're well intended. If he or she agrees with you, fine. But if they don't agree, you should continue your neutral role. If the situation worsens, revisit the discussion.

Part 2: The Supportive Spouse Dilemma: A Typical Scenario

My husband works harder than anyone else in his family, so why isn't he treated fairly?

My husband and his two brothers have worked with their father in the family business for 10 years. I'm glad his job is secure, but I know it's not so easy to work with family. That's why I make sure I'm involved when I need to be. You've got to protect your own household's turf or the others in the family will run right over you. I know I've ruffled a few feathers, so I'm making a special effort today at the family dinner to be pleasant to everyone, even my sister-in-law, the one who hates the family, and, no doubt, me! Sure enough, as we enter the backyard, I see her sitting alone reading a magazine.

After getting through the pleasantries, she glances at our husbands and their father in a huddle discussing business. "It's like this every time we get together. Why don't they just meet at the office and save the weekend for us? I can't believe my father-in-law can look my husband in the face. Does Dad treat him like a partner, as he had promised? No! He's so smart, yet no one in this family appreciates it. If it weren't for him, the business wouldn't be where it is today. I think he'd be better off somewhere else."

Remembering my goal to be pleasant, I decide not to tell her what I really think and instead say, "I'm sure things will work out once they decide who's in charge of what."

She wasn't buying it. "I've heard that before," she said. "It's all just a ploy. I'd rather move back home and let him get started somewhere else. I could see my family more often. Maybe this family will realize his value once he's gone."

"Listen," I pulled up a chair. " When my husband got the shaft from his father last year I marched right over to the office and gave Dad a piece of my mind."

"So what happened?" she asked.

"I got what I wanted–for them to give my husband more money and more responsibility."

"Wow," she said. "You're good." Actually, I wasn't. They gave him more responsibility, but not more money, and

I managed to alienate my father-in-law to the point that he barely grunts hello to me.

I don't get it. If you stay detached and keep the complaints to yourself, like my sister-in-law, nothing happens. If you become involved and try to champion your spouse, like I did, you end up burning bridges. So, what's a wife supposed to do when she sees her husband struggling?

What's the Supportive Spouse Thinking?

Married to the mob, an outsider looking in–that's how a lot of wives feel when their husbands work for the family business. There's nowhere to turn, nobody to ask, nothing they can do. The anger, frustration, and resentment build to the point where they become either paralyzed by the feeling of helplessness or destructive with the need for justice.

These powerful feelings tend to split spouses into three kinds of partners:

1. **The Can't-Be-Bothered Wife.** This Spouse keeps marriage and the family business separate. Her life is so busy she just doesn't pay that much attention to the family soap opera. Usually she has her own career, or is perpetually involved with the kids and other activities. When her husband has business-related troubles, she listens, gives advice, and goes on with her life.
2. **The Bitter Bitch.** She's resentful and vocal with hubby about how poorly he's treated. Believing her hubby is smarter, more dedicated, and more valuable than everyone else, Spouse usually

delivers a constant loop of "Can't they see things your way? Why don't they appreciate you?" Or, "You're better than them!" She usually votes for leaving the family business or, if he has shares, selling it so they can take the money and run. Unable to control her emotions, she has negative discussions with the in-laws, usually resulting in her being marginalized even further.

3. **The Buttinsky.** This spouse butts into everything whether she's justified or not. She sees herself as part cheerleader/part offensive tackle. Emphasis on "offensive." When hubby is troubled, it's her mission to fix it. She talks, or, more bluntly, stalks the relatives, often browbeating them. She's *sometimes* a positive influence, but always a pain in the ass.

Which Spouse are you? Notice how wildly different they are, yet they all have one thing in common–they're almost completely ineffective in advancing their own agenda. Partly because they're using counter-productive tactics and partly because spouses often feel they don't have the right to say anything. After all, if you're just "the wife" you should keep your trap shut, right? You'll often get an unspoken message from your in-laws: "The family business was here before you came along, and with the 50 percent divorce rate, it'll be around after you're tossed aside."

There may be a lot of truth to that, but after years of *being* the in-laws and *dealing* with in-laws, we can tell you this: You have far more power than you think–you're just not using it in the right way. In this chapter, we'll show you how to use the tremendous influence you didn't know you had in a way that nobody in the family thought you could.

Four Action Steps for the Supportive Spouse

Action Step #1

Become a "Supportive Spouse."

Change your spousal style. Ditch the Can't-Be-Bothered, Bitter Bitch, and Buttinsky roles and embrace a new one: Supportive Spouse. She's strong, smart, and diplomatic. She recognizes that the source of her power is the bond she has with her husband. Most wives think their husbands are smarter, more talented, and contribute more than anyone else in the family business. Husbands appreciate that, and that's what makes spouses so powerful. Who doesn't listen to the person who always takes your side? By offering perspective, advice, and consolation, the Supportive Spouse is the husband's de facto business partner.

Supportive Spouse knows that her marriage gives her a legitimate say in how her husband is treated. Whether the family likes it or not, she is a stakeholder in their business. It affects her financial well-being, her children's future, her social life, her reputation, and, of course, her spouse's career.

In our view, you don't have the right to express your opinions and influence the business–you have an obligation.

Action Step #2

Learn about the who, what, where, and when.

If you didn't grow up in a family business, it's worth the effort to learn as much as you can about this unique blend of power, blood, and money. Whether it's by reading books such as this one or investigating the family business programs at the local college, you'll be better prepared to deal with the issues you and your spouse are facing. Although most books on family business don't cover in-laws in depth, just understanding more about the general subject will be helpful. You'll quickly find out the issues you're facing are more common than you think.

After you've learned family business basics, you'll need a lesson on your spouse's family business–but not from your spouse. Why? Because he's too close to it. Sure, you need to know his perspective, but if you really want to be effective, get everyone else's. You'll be amazed how family members can view the very same situation in very different ways. Start by asking your father- or mother-in-law to give you the low-down on the past. Your goal? To learn about the roles that were established in the past, so you can better understand the present and predict the future.

Let's say you've always wondered why Uncle Jim is untouchable at the office when he's clearly not pulling his weight. After a long lunch with your mother-in-law, you learn that 15 years ago, Uncle Jim saved the business from bankruptcy. He put his own savings into it and asked for nothing in return. The family's genuine sense of gratitude for pulling the business out of its tailspin netted him lifetime squatting rights at the corner office and a "Do Not Touch" sign that exempts him from proving his worth.

This invaluable lesson shows two common phenomena in family businesses: a family member who once rescued the business and now adds nothing to it, and a business culture that rewards loyalty more than it does performance. We're sure your husband's business has these or other stories in its history. Learn as much as you can, and you'll understand the undercurrents that make the surface look so strange.

Action Step #3

Draw your own conclusions.

How do you see the family business? Through your husband's eyes, of course. He's your direct link, the filter through which all news from the office must travel. Does he come home complaining that his sister is a slacker? That his brother is a moron? That his Dad is too old for the job? Does he tell you he's not appreciated and no one listens to him? With all the complaining, it's easy to grow resentful of his family. Before you put on your Wonder Woman outfit to take on his world, find out if your husband's gripes are legitimate, because if they're not, even your golden lariat won't save the day.

Start probing a little when hubby starts venting. It's your marital privilege. Cash in on your relationships with other family members or employees and ask their opinions without generating suspicion. Does he work as hard as he'd like everyone to believe? Are his decisions usually overturned? Who really reports to him and how does he spend his day? What are his responsibilities compared to other family members and employees? Does he have legitimate beefs with the family or should he be happy to get a paycheck?

You may come back thinking he's just blowing off steam with the only person he can, and that all is well at the office. In this case, listen to him, but don't let it affect your relationship with the family.

You may also come back thinking his beefs aren't legitimate and they're really a smoke screen for his shortcomings, which explains why his father, in an effort to keep peace, put him on the rubber gun squad. If that's the case, be grateful his family is taking care of him and turn your attention to something more productive.

On the other hand, your reconnaissance mission might uncover that your husband's claims are legitimate, and that the family is truly taking advantage of him. Now what? Typically, husband and family are headed for an iceberg with no one willing to change course. How can you help?

If you believe your husband could use some independent input, do your own research to find an advisor, set an appointment, and go with him (we're big on family business consultants, can you tell? Mostly because, if we'd used them early on, we probably wouldn't have had to sell our businesses).Then, follow the next step.

Action Step #4

Be helpful.

If conflict in your husband's family is a regular occurrence, you'll always be walking a tightrope. Learn how to balance yourself or you'll keep falling off, and no doubt landing on your least favorite in-law. So how do you know when to step in and when to stay out? Trial and error. You can't play career counselor, family therapist, and advocate for hubby every time there's a hiccup in the family business, but you can learn how to handle some common conflicts without ruffling feathers. The trick is to match your actions with your intentions. This is harder than you think when you're swirling in a sea of emotions, so we've laid out a few common mistakes Supportive Spouses make and how they can correct them.

Matching Perception With Intention

Situation	You think you're helping by...	You'd be better off...
Husband and Dad had a disagreement at work. Now he doesn't want to attend a social function with Dad.	Agreeing and calling to cancel.	Suggesting they leave the issue at the office and try to enjoy each other as family.
Your mother-in-law wants you to help broker peace between your husband and his brother who are rivals at work.	Telling her you like to keep your marriage and the family business separate and don't want to get involved.	Realizing she recognizes your status in the family and discussing with her ways to help.
Husband and siblings can't agree on anything in the business.	Taking his side and joining in the negativity about his siblings.	Suggesting he learn more about resolving conflicts among siblings at the local college's family business program.

Chapter Summary

In-Laws Under the Influence

For the Son-in-Law: If you're thinking about joining your wife's family business or you're already there, here's a summary of our two Action Steps:

- **Action Step #1:** Don't join unless you are invited. If the family pursues you, consider the offer and be sure to review all of the pluses and minuses with your spouse.
- **Action Step #2:** Put the issues on the table before you get on the payroll. Have a lawyer, with expertise in family business, advise you on the key legal issues. If you join, you'll need to set some stringent rules with the family and your spouse.

For the Supportive Spouse: If your husband works in his family's business, here's a summary of our recommendations to become a Supportive Spouse.

- **Action Step #1:** Change your spousal style from Can't-Be-Bothered, Bitter Bitch, or Buttinsky. You are your husband's de facto business partner. Become the Supportive Spouse.
- **Action Step #2:** Learn about family businesses so you're better prepared to deal with the issues you and your spouse are facing.
- **Action Step #3:** Draw you own conclusions about how your husband is treated in the family business. Do your own investigation.
- **Action Step #4:** Learn to handle some of the common conflicts without ruffling any feathers.

The Father With Farewell Paranoia

It's a lot easier to start a business than it is to let go of it. Whether it's the fear of the business sliding or the fear of your grip slipping, paranoia and angst rule a father's day. That's why this chapter is devoted to the two monumental issues every father in a family business will face: succession and retirement.

If you're a father reading this section, you'll see we've given voice to all your hopes and fears about letting go and selecting your replacement. Our goal is to comfort you with a realistic plan and safeguards to keep the business on track as you begin a new phase of life. If you're someone working with Father (Dad), we'll help you understand why it's so difficult for him to step aside and what you can do to ease the process. And no, it doesn't involve throwing him down the stairs. It involves helping him work through his worries and concerns.

No matter who you are, you'll have more appreciation for the questions dads ask themselves, the fears they have to face, and the planning needed to get through this difficult period. We'll start with a typical scenario, then move to our personal observations and insights. We'll finish with practical advice and Action Steps to help you, Dad, determine when it's time to retire, plan your transition out of the day-to-day business, and most importantly, how to make sure it's set up so the family and the business will continue to prosper.

Chapter 5

The Farewell Dilemma: A Typical Scenario

Am I ready to let go? How do I pick my replacement?

I've been in this meeting for an hour and my bladder's about to burst! Doesn't anybody else have to go to the bathroom? And look at this new customer–he's so young he could be my son! Is it my imagination, or are all my customers at least 30 years younger than I am?

My wife used to love hearing about the business. Now she just yawns. She wants to travel more but I keep telling her I can't take that much time off. The other night we had a terrible fight. "What was the point of bringing the kids into the business if you're not going to relax more and enjoy life?" she screamed. "If we wait much longer we'll be traveling with a nurse! The answer is simple: Turn over more responsibility to the kids so you can take more time off!"

My son must have heard the screaming across town. Yesterday, he said he was ready to take on more responsibility. He's already second in command. The only position left is mine.

My friends aren't helping. Our scores were all pretty even when we started out golfing together. Now that they're all retired or semi-retired, I'm stuck at a 20 handicap and they're down to a 10. "Get out of the office," they said, "it'll improve your game."

I don't know...maybe they all have a point, but I can't imagine not being in the office everyday. I started this business 30 years ago with nothing but determination and hard work. I am this company and it's all I know. What would I do? I can't play golf everyday. That's for old people.

If I did consider pulling back from the business, who's going to take my place? I've got a son, a daughter, and a son-in-law in the business–each with pluses and minuses. What would our long-term managers think if I started working less? Would they get nervous about the changes and leave the company? Would they work less?

The thing that worries me the most is my nest egg. I worked hard for what I built. Can I depend on others if I'm not involved in the day-to-day? Will they be as diligent as I am? I keep thinking that turning over control of the company means losing control of my income. I keep picturing my replacement making some stupid mistake or taking an outrageous risk, ruining the business and setting the stage for my new career as a Wal-Mart greeter.

I don't want to die at my desk, but I can't pass the baton yet. There's got to be some middle ground, but I can't figure out what it is.

What's Father Thinking?

Father is at a crossroads. Does he stay? Does he leave? Friends, family, and trusted confidants are dropping so many hints it feels like it's raining clues. So why is it so hard for him to let go?

First, the business is his lifetime achievement. He's sacrificed everything for it–vacations, friendships, time with his family, and more. He built the company, put food on the table, money in the bank, and when business boomed, a new car in the garage. But more than financial success, the business always provided him with purpose and identity. To this day, everyone comes to him for direction, for budget approval, for answers. He likes the power of being in charge and the esteem that comes from success. He's involved in the community. He's been the face of the company for years. He speaks at civic events, sponsors charity auctions, and donates services to the schools. Will Dad, the go-to guy, become a has-been without the company throne? Dad is stalling the inevitable, in part because he's afraid of losing his identity. He's not sure of his ability to be alone with himself or to be at home with little to do. For Dad, retiring feels more like giving up more than it does letting go.

Yes, he'd love to take it easier, travel a little more, and get down to a 10 handicap like the rest of his buddies. But his ego keeps taunting him: "If I'm not in charge what's going to happen to the company? What am I going to do all day if I'm not at the office? Is the community still going to pay attention to what I say and do?"

Dad may have ego issues, but they pale in comparison to his other worry: his financial future. Dad has a very real concern about the viability of the business when he's not around. With most of his wealth tied up in the business, the thought of someone else making risky business decisions scares the hell out of him. Will his replacement miss an important shift in the industry? Will he maintain the same customer service and employee retention? Will current customers continue to do business with the company once Dad steps down? What if the family implodes in a war for power and ruins the business? No, no, no. Dad's right to worry. Leaving could be the reckless gamble of a lifetime.

Eeny, Meeny, Miny, Mo

How do you pick the person to replace you? It's gut-wrenching enough to admit that you should be moving on, but to anoint the person who is going to sit in your chair? That's hard. What's even harder is telling the other family candidates they didn't get your job. How do you tell your eldest son you picked his baby sister to lead the company? Selecting your replacement can be an emotionally explosive event if you don't manage it carefully. That's why we've developed a long-term plan to guide you through it.

Depending on the family talent pool, choosing your successor can be a breeze or a blowout. Dad may feel that he has no good choices in his family or the company. Maybe he can't imagine that anyone can do the job he's done, so why consider leaving? Other Dads are just too afraid of gambling on the existing team's abilities. If the future requires a new investment, he probably doesn't want the added risk. A "moving aside" date keeps moving further away, because he just doesn't have confidence the company can survive without him.

Alternatively, Dad may have a terrific bench–a promising son, a brilliant daughter, or an ever-dependable professional manager. But that, too, has its problems. Everybody in the family has their own ideas of who should or shouldn't take over, adding to Dad's pressure. These aren't just ordinary succession issues. The wrong choice–or even the right choice–has the potential for splitting the family apart and putting the business at risk. Believe us, we know. We can trace many of our family-related issues to Dad's retirement. If you're not careful about your succession plan you may ignite a family brawl that will bring down the company.

On the following pages, you'll find out how to avoid the catastrophes we just mentioned. You'll learn how to tell if you're ready to let go, how to make the transition at your own pace, why you should consider the not-so-obvious candidates, and, most helpful, the questions you should be asking yourself during every stage of the transition. Our three-step strategy will help your company prosper after you leave and help your family work together for the common good.

Three Action Steps for the Father With Farewell Paranoia

Action Step #1

Find out where you are in the letting-go process.

Self-reflection is your first step. Spend time during a weekend or vacation when you're free from distractions to take your Retirement Temperature. Are you frozen in place with no chance of moving or burning up with exit fever? Only you can decide, but here are some of the questions you need to ask yourself:

- Has the business begun to bore you?
- Are you starting to yell "run!" instead of "charge!" when you see an obstacle?
- Are you spending more time reading the *Wall Street Journal* than the weekly management reports?
- Are you resisting the idea of expanding the business and taking on debt?
- Have all your friends migrated south looking healthier and tanner than you?
- Did you stop attending the national trade shows?

- Do you put the industry trade magazine in your "bathroom reading" basket?
- Has it been more than a couple of months since you've seen your top customers?
- Can you find anything to do after 2 p.m.?
- Do you attend meetings without your hearing aid, miss what was said, and make a decision anyway?

If your answers to these questions make you realize you've got one foot out the door, but one foot stuck inside, go to Step #2. We've got the perfect glue remover.

On the other hand, if your answers convince you that you're nowhere near ready to retire, that's great–unless you're between 60 and 65 years old. If you are, you've got a couple of camouflaged land mines ahead of you: Family members who know you're still capable of running the ship, but resent your unwillingness to acknowledge that you eventually won't; professional managers who think their careers are going nowhere because you're going to die at your desk.

In other words, even if you're perfectly capable, willing, and able to continue captaining the ship into your 70s you *still* have to discuss succession, start the grooming process, and give more responsibility to more people, or you're going to hear "Man overboard!" a lot more than you'll want.

For beginners, start a conversation. Set expectations. Be honest. Say, "I'm nowhere near ready to retire, but I also recognize that we've got to start the succession process. I'd like to give more responsibilities to more people so that when I am ready to retire I can do it with complete confidence." Remember this fact and it will make your conversations easier: Studies show that family businesses with longer transition periods have a greater chance of surviving to the next generation.

An International Example

Sometimes It's Beyond Your Control

Thailand's Dhanin Chearavanont, patriarch of the $13-billion agribusiness giant Charoen Pokphavian Group, told *Time* magazine he'd like to retire, but things keep cropping up at work, such as the 1997 Asian financial meltdown that forced him to sell assets to repay $400 million in bank debt. Or the avian flu scare that disrupted the Thai poultry industry. His three sons are waiting in the wings, but the 65-plus chairman is waiting for things to calm down.

The Big Point

Delegate and Stay Delegated

As you phase yourself out, make sure everyone knows who is boss when you're not there. Employees can get confused when hearing from multiple bosses. If you've delegated administration to your nephew during your absence, don't call your financial manager directly to see how the quarterly report and monthly billing are coming. Speak with your nephew and funnel your concerns and questions through him.

Action Step #2

Create a "Triple-5" plan addressing your needs at ages 55, 60, and 65

We know it's hard to think about, let alone develop, succession plans when you're steeped in day-to-day business. That's why we've done it for you. Our Triple-5 plan is the perfect way to make sure the keys of your kingdom land in the right hands. Our approach uses three five-year intervals beginning on your 55th birthday. Why five-year intervals? It's about the longest period of time you can reasonably forecast. Our approach is based on the idea that the three things everybody wants in life don't just happen—you have to make them happen: Time to do what you want, the money to do it with, and the control to manage it. Our Triple-5 plan helps you in all three areas by suggesting what to think and do at every five-year interval.

What You Should Be Thinking and Doing at Age 55

What's your business worth?

Get an outside appraisal. Appraisers will estimate the value of your company under different scenarios, typically using recent sales transactions in your industry, called "comps," and the cash flow from your company. Appraisals give you a range of values useful to planning your financial future. In our case, it was helpful to learn the industry benchmarks for the company's valuation in estate planning and what buyers find attractive.

Is all your money in the business?

Ours was. And if you're similar to most Dads, yours is too. Fortunately, we had the foresight to hire a financial planner who helped us diversify. Diversification is important because, if you are similar to many owners, and want to "gift" stock to your family, it means you have less of the one asset you own. Not a good position for you. There's a saying that poor men buy hubcaps, middle-income men buy cars, and rich men buy appreciating assets. Translation? Invest like the rich. Buy something that will make you money–such as real estate and insurance. And don't forget to set up your 401(k).

The Big Point

Put Another "S" in Your Asset

If your business is your only asset, it's time to diversify. Here are two ideas:

Real Estate

Pay rent to yourself instead of your landlord. Ask your lawyer to set up a separate company, owned by you, to purchase a building that your company moves into. With the company as the tenant, you should get a mortgage relatively easily.

Life Insurance

Life insurance is an asset that can be used in a variety of ways in a family business. As Dad, a policy on your life can be used to pay your estate for your shares in the company that you can pass to the kids. It can also be sold in the marketplace. Don't put this off until you're too old to pass the medical exam.

How much do you need to retire?

Family business owners have to think differently about retirement than executives at public companies. It doesn't make any sense to burden the family business with paying your full salary after you've retired. The more responsibility you relinquish the less you should be making. You've got other problems, too. You're not getting a pension from IBM. You don't have Boeing's benefits plan. You can't go to GE's Human Resources department. In fact, there's nowhere to go but the mirror. And that's why you must take responsibility for your own retirement. Do what we did and you'll never regret it: Hire financial planners and make them your best friends. They'll ask the tough questions, force you to think strategically, and offer innovative solutions.

Categorize: Suspects, Prospects, and Candidates

Sort out your successor by categorizing your kids and other family members into three possibilities: (1) Suspects (they've got a pulse and know their name), (2) Prospects (they're working at the company, perform well, and seem to know where the bathrooms are), and (3) Candidates (they've done the heavy lifting and are seriously qualified to carry you out of the corner office). At the Suspect stage, your kids are probably in their 20s, close to finishing their education, or have already started a career. Are you interested in having them join you? Are there other family members you want in the business? If not, we see a For Sale sign hanging on your company door in the not-too-distant future.

Execute a Will

Eighty percent of your counterparts have done it by the time they turned 50 years old. Have you? If you haven't, do it *now* so you can protect your wealth and take advantage of the generous but complex tax laws. A will, along with an estate plan, are without exception the most important documents you can put in place. You don't want most of what you've worked for confiscated by the IRS or held in probate until your case shows up on the court calendar.

Form an outside advisory council

It should include your accountants, lawyers, peers, and family business consultants. Meet at least once a year. They'll help you clarify and resolve any issues that come up at this stage of the transition.

Develop interests outside of the company

An odd thing to say, we know, but you won't believe how much easier it will be to let go of the reins if you have hobbies, sports, or charitable work about which you feel passionate. Remember the three things everybody wants–time, money, and control? What good will they do if you're spending the day in a bathrobe? Don't wait until you are 65 years old to develop interests–it will make your succession plan very difficult.

What You Should Be Thinking and Doing at Age 60

Your personal financial plan and wealth diversification

Dust off the financial plan you made five years ago. Are your assumptions still the same? Has the value of the business changed? Review your asset diversification progress. Think of it as going to the doctor for a check-up even though nothing is wrong. While you're getting that check-up, get a second opinion. Have a new financial planner review the strategies your current financial planners put in place.

Have Suspects turned into Prospects?

Your children should be around 30 years old now. Do they have the skills or potential to help you maintain or grow the business? Can you work with them? Is it enjoyable? If so, you should be actively mentoring their career as they take senior roles in the company.

Do you want to give your kids the business?

If so, it's probably time to consider transferring stock to them. If your kids have made a commitment to your business and you answered yes to all the previous questions, talk to your tax accountant and your lawyer. You can minimize the tax bite of passing the stock to family in a number of ways. In our case, Dad divided his shares into voting and nonvoting classes, passing ("gifting") the nonvoting shares, at a discounted value. Through time, we received a substantial amount of the value of the company's stock, while my father retained the majority of voting shares. The timing of the gifting process is different for each family business. My father began gifting stock when he was in his 60s and it was clear that we were seriously committed to the business. Here are some considerations: the amount of wealth you have outside of the business, current vs. future tax benefits, your health, the family's performance in the business, and length of time the family has spent as managers in the company.

Should you give stock to kids who don't work in the business?

Your intent may be to "treat the kids equally," but the result may be to alienate them forever. On the one hand, you shouldn't punish children who pursue a different career path by withholding stock from them. The same goes for kids who choose to become stay-at-home moms or dads. On the other hand, you shouldn't punish children who joined the family business by diluting their ownership and putting them in a position of enriching their brothers and sisters who chose not to work in the business. A worker-bee sister putting in 14-hour days is not going to be happy that she made her stay-at-home brother a millionaire. By the same token, the worker-bee sister, as a majority owner, could block a stay-at-home brother's desire to cash in his shares to pay for his children's education, causing enormous anger.

We understand your desire to bond the kids together with a shared legacy, but, remember, the path to family business feuds is paved with good intentions. If you decide to gift stock to all your children, be sure to amend your shareholder agreement to provide favorable options for every conceivable scenario.

The Big Point

Give So It Doesn't Hurt

Consider giving stock to the kids working in the family business and other assets to the kids who aren't, for example, your home, income-producing real estate, or life insurance.

Make money with money

At this point, you're not just making money with the sweat of your brow or the size of your salary, right? Our asset diversification strategy should have injected steroids into your nest egg by now. Whether it's appreciation in real estate holdings or a doubling of mutual funds, you should be using money to make money from here on out, even when you're sleeping.

What You Should Be Thinking and Doing at Age 65

Move out of the day-day-day operations S-L-O-W-L-Y

At your own speed, shift yourself out of the day-to-day activities. It's a signal that the transition has begun in earnest. There's no need to rush. You're the boss; you set the pace. A well-planned phase-out eases everyone into their new roles and reduces anxieties that uncertainty can bring.

Begin by writing down your responsibilities at work. How do you spend your day? Do you run all of the management meetings? Are you the primary account representative for some clients? Do expenditures need approval from you? Are you the contact for the company's accountants, lawyers, insurance representatives, and bankers? Can you assign some duties to another manager or family member today? Can the remainder be delegated through time? If so, make the assignments and provide a realistic timetable to turn over the responsibilities while you're still in the driver's seat. That way you can see if your management team is up for the job.

To delegate or not. That is the question. Yes is the answer. It's still your basketball, but let other people bounce it. So delegate, delegate, delegate. Come in at 10 a.m. and leave at 2 p.m. You're setting the stage for succession by signaling that it'll come within the next six to 12 months. Start grooming candidates (see next section) and make sure everyone knows who they are. This is an important point: your successor should not be a surprise to anyone! The best way to avoid family brawls is to avoid surprises. Make the succession completely transparent from beginning to end.

Start a "shadowing" program with the people you've assigned to take over some of your duties. Bring them in and let them observe you in action. By shadowing you, they'll learn how you operate in different settings. Is your son going to take over your banking relationships? Introduce him to the bankers, let him join you at banking meetings, and review your company's banking agreements and covenants together. Is your daughter the new manager of your larger customers? Bring her in on all the customer service problems, the new pricing strategy, and the monthly lunches you enjoy with the customers.

Talk up the transition; don't keep it a secret. Employees get nervous when they see changes without explanations. Transparency relieves anxiety. If you want to decrease disruptions increase discussions. You might want to begin your transition by working a four-day week or leaving the office at two in the afternoon. Tell your staff. Let your words pave the path to your actions.

Get out of town. Once you've gotten used to your new schedule, consider taking extended vacations once, twice, even more times during the year. In our own business, Dad continued to move further away from day-to-day management by spending months away at a second home. It provided a clear signal to everyone we had committed to a transition. When he returned for meetings or a few weeks during the summer, customers and employees could see the continuity in the business while the new team had the confidence to grow in new directions.

Most family businesses make the transition throughout a period of years. The beauty of a slow transition is that you can correct failures as they happen so they don't become systemic. If you don't like what you see at the company when you return from an extended time away, you have the ability to make more changes.

The Big Point

Move it, don't schmooze it. Don't just talk about moving out of daily management, do it. Here's how you'll know you've actually begun to let go:

- You see there's a management meeting and, instead of joining it, you walk by and wave.
- When a manager brings you a problem to solve you reply, *'What did my son say?'*

Have Prospects turned into Candidates?

By now, at least one of your kids or family members should have grown from Suspect to Prospect to Candidate. Whether you have one, many, or none, here are a few candidate options you should consider:

➡ **My Daughter, CEO.** Women have often gotten the short end of the stick in family businesses, but that's changing. Even in male-dominated industries, daughters are often running the family businesses. Unfortunately, the biggest obstacle to My Daughter the CEO isn't her brother, sister, employee, or client; it's Dad. He often has a hard time envisioning his little girl in the boss's chair. He may want grandchildren, and if he makes her CEO, she might choose to delay having kids. Or, Dad may be concerned about how his upper management–most often, male–will react. He knows they'll be polite, but will they respect her or undermine her? Will they get behind her or leave the company? How will his sons feel?

While these may be legitimate concerns, they're not serious enough to keep you from putting your qualified, capable daughter in the driver's seat. A recent study showed 34 percent of family businesses expected their next CEO to be female, and of those expecting two or more co-CEOS in the future, nearly half indicate one of the CEOs may be female. The same study showed female-run family businesses have less family attrition and are more productive than their male-run counterparts. My Daughter the CEO may turn out to be My Daughter the Company's Salvation.

An International Example

A Woman in Turkey

Guler Sabani, arguably the most powerful woman in Turkey, heads the Turkish industrial giant, Sabanci Group. Described by employees as "tough" and "unpretentious," Guler was chosen by her uncle to succeed him over her two brothers and many male offspring.

- **Co-CEOs.** Consider forming an "Office of the President." It's perfect for the company that has two or more family members who get along, have specific responsibilities, and compatible competencies. When the need for expertise in multiple disciplines grows, two heads are often better than one.

  Family business advisors report this is a new, powerful, though untested trend. Until recently, only 5–10 percent of family businesses operated with co-CEOs running the show. But surveys reveal approximately 40–50 percent of family businesses anticipate co-ownership and co-management by a group of siblings in the future. If you're lucky enough to have family members who work well together, why not suggest that they continue to work as a team? Let them divide responsibilities and reporting lines.

- **Non-family.** Your family isn't ready, willing, or able, it's time to reach across bloodlines and hire a non-family professional. He or she may already be part of your management team or working for a competitor. They may even be a top officer at your biggest competitor.

  This is a good option for Dads with young or inexperienced family in the business who may eventually assume the top position. Another plus: a professional may be able to manage through rapid change or growth when Dad's skills are lacking and he can't provide the mentoring the family needs for the future.

An International Example

Hired Hand in France

Jean-Louis Dumas, member of the founding family at Hermes, International, brought in an external co-CEO, Patrick Thomas, to help transition through a succession period. The French luxury goods powerhouse had several family members at the company, but no obvious single heir. Thomas expects to step down with Dumas when the new team is in place.

- **Let Them Decide, CEO.** If you have kids in the business and have confidence in their judgment, consider letting them decide who should be your successor–it's their problem in the long run anyway! Give them three months and a consultant or company advisor to help guide them. Here, you avoid the conflicts that arise when you make the selection unilaterally. By taking this route, you are letting the future stakeholders decide who should run the company.
- **In-law CEO.** Selecting a son- or daughter-in-law to run the business? What, are we crazy? Not really. We know the possibility of a divorce makes this option a nightmare scenario. We know how difficult it would be to separate your children's

feelings from your business, but we also know there are great examples of multi-generational family businesses that have selected in-laws to run the company, such as the *New York Times.* When your in-law brings a lot to the table, why not consider him or her?

If you do have in-laws capable of running the business you'll face a sensitive question: Should you give them stock? The answer will vary from family to family, but we feel that if an in-law has shown commitment to the business *and* the family throughout the years, you should reward him or her with stock ownership.

Announce your successor

Again, it shouldn't be a surprise, but it's important that you have some kind of ritual that cements the change and strongly communicates that this person was indeed your pick. Consider having a company-sponsored "inaugural" dinner or a quick announcement in the conference room with a cake to enjoy.

Keep your eyes on the business, but your hands off the wheel

We don't suggest that you completely disengage from the company. Bump yourself up to Chairman of the Board. That way you can keep tabs on the direction of the company and consult with the managers on any major changes. Be sure to receive only the management reports that give you a global perspective, and, if something alarms you, ask your successor about it. If you need more assurance, attend a staff meeting.

But here's the trick: Attend it, don't call it. Don't neuter your new anointment. Subverting your successor is bad for business. Let *them* call the meeting. Being a chairman at age 65 sets the stage for having one foot in and one foot out.

Action Step #3

Install a board of directors.

We know all of the excuses for not having a Board of Directors. We used them too:

- We don't want to be legally bound by the board's decisions.
- We don't want outsiders to know our compensation, net worth, estate plans, succession plans, company dirty laundry, family dirty laundry, etc.
- We don't want to pay the insurance for the board members.
- We don't want to answer to anyone but ourselves.
- We don't want to be embarrassed when outsiders see the patients are running the institution.

Throw away all these excuses and take our advice: If you're the Father With Farewell Paranoia, there's no better way to make sure that the family and company management are held accountable in the family business than taking this step. Think of it as bringing a new sheriff into town, just in case Billy the Kid rides in.

If you followed our recommendation to set up an outside council of advisors, you've had a few years to see the benefits of an outsider's perspective on the business. Creating a Board of Directors is a natural evolution that gives your company more stature and professionalism. That's exactly what you'll need at this stage of the business if you want to keep the family legacy going.

Chapter Summary

The Father With Farewell Paranoia

Are you ready to let go and pick your successor? Here is the summary of our plan:

- **Action step #1:** Take your retirement temperature by answering our list of questions. Know where you stand in the letting go process.
- **Action step #2:** Create a Triple-5 transition plan addressing your needs at ages 55, 60, and 65. This includes knowing how much your business is worth, how much you need to retire, categorizing your kids into Suspects, Prospects, and Candidates, forming an advisory council, and more. It also includes moving out of the day-to-day operations s-l-o-w-l-y and making the succession plan completely transparent.
- **Action step #3:** Install a formal Board of Directors. It will keep everyone, family or not, accountable to the business.

Chapter 6

The Sibling Rivals

"MY MOM'S HAVING A BABY. THAT AUTOMATICALLY MOVES ME INTO A MIDDLE MANAGEMENT CAPACITY WITHIN THE FAMILY INFRASTRUCTURE."

Even airlines don't handle as much of a family's baggage as brothers and sisters do. They say they love each other, but they'll fight for the money, prestige, and power in the family business at the drop of a hat. If a brother gets promoted faster it's because Dad always loved him best. If a sister gets better sales territory, it's because she outfoxed him. When Brother is outvoted 3 to 1 on his new business proposal, it's because the other sibs plotted against him.

These are everyday occurrences with Sibling Rivals, and they put the company in jeopardy. Nothing good can come to a business when judgment is clouded by emotions. If your business is groaning under the strain of brothers and sisters who can't work together, there's a very good chance you're going to end up with a golden goose that only lays scrambled eggs.

We'll help you stop, minimize, or neutralize the behavior that can bring down a family business faster than a meteor stamped "special delivery" to earth. In this chapter, we'll identify the root causes of sibling rivalry, how to keep them in check, and how to get everyone to keep their eye on the donut and not on the hole.

Though we're addressing this chapter to siblings, we strongly recommend you hand this chapter to Mom and Dad, who, whether they know it or not, are probably main characters in the Sibling Soap Opera. They are going to be key players in many of our recommendations.

The Sibling Rival's Dilemma: A Typical Scenario

How can I work with my brothers and sisters without losing my sanity?

My brother, sister, and I just don't get along at work. Dad dreams about passing down the business to us, but I'm afraid we'll wreck it if we don't start working together.

My little brother has always been competitive, but he's gotten out of control. His latest escapade took money out of my pocket. He asked for my help on a proposal to a new customer then cut me out of the presentation. He just shrugged when I confronted him. I said, "Hey, you couldn't have won the account without my help–why wasn't I invited to the presentation?" I'm convinced the only reason he didn't include me was so he didn't have to share the commission.

This brought my sister into the mess. She runs administration at the company and processes the commission checks. "He told me you didn't add much to the deal and the commission is all his," she says after I marched into her office looking for my check. "How could you take his side without even asking me?" I yelled.

"You know the rules. Maybe you should've been at the presentation," she snapped back.

Last Friday was the final straw. For the quarterly management presentation, my brother insisted on last-minute edits and handed out the presentation at the meeting. It had recommendations on how he would increase sales by opening a new office. He knows I don't agree, but put it in the presentation behind my back.

Who does he think he is? Is he trying to convince Dad that he should take over after he retires? He's wasting his time–I'm the oldest and have the most experience in the company.

I know I've done my share to contribute to this mess, but it has to end. Everyone's missing the point, we're family. It's just a matter of time before we start doing real damage to the company. But how do I stop it?

What Are the Sibling Rivals Thinking?

The Sibling Rivals have had the same thought since childhood: How can I make my parents see that I'm "the one"–the one they like best, the one they trust most, the one they're most proud of. It's all about that endorsement from Mom and Dad or anyone else with an opinion. The message is simple: judge us and pick me.

When they were fighting about who got the top bunk bed, it was annoying, but inconsequential. Now their rivalry has spilled over into the family business and the family nest egg hangs in the balance. Can't they grow up and realize they're on the same team? Why are they still fighting for a parent's approval instead of building the business and worrying about the competition?

To put it simply: money, power, and prestige. Who will make the most money? Who will be chosen for that coveted title and position once Parent retires? Who will be "the decider"? In many family businesses, the top of the money-power-prestige triangle is determined by birth order. The oldest is the de facto replacement to run the company when Parent steps down. If the sibs agree and fall in line behind him or her, the company winds up out of the woods. If the sibs aren't convinced, the company often winds up in the weeds.

Is sibling strife always a predictor of a family business failure? No. Some siblings, despite their rivalry, manage to get along and can work together productively. Why? They've found the key to success: they genuinely like and enjoy each other. Sure, they've had conflicts in the past, but they're not going to cancel their regular tennis match together next Sunday, much less let a disagreement disrupt the business or their relationship. The family business is in greater jeopardy when left in the hands of sibs together only because Dad's around, and that's where the power and money are. Without that connection to make them want to work it out, their partnership is doomed.

The Parent Trap

Unfortunately, some parents consciously or unconsciously provoke the siblings, causing further strain. Instead of encouraging them to act as one independent unit, Parent praises or "showcases" one sibling over the other. So, Parent stays in control while taunting the siblings with the dangling carrot–recognition and a shot at the big prize (the presidency). When the tension has everyone at the company and at home on edge, Parent comes to the rescue with band-aid solutions. Here are a few that may sound familiar:

- **The "Go to your corner" strategy:** Here, Parent separates the Sibling Rivals by giving them different operating areas, territories, or business functions. The problem with this seemingly bright idea is that the sibs will create their own fiefdoms inside the business. If all they care about are their own respective silos, how will they decide what's best for the company as a whole? Yes, it's a short-term solution, but it works only as long as Parent's around. Parent's retirement can bring down the house of cards.
- **The sooth-and-smooth technique:** Here, Parent attempts nip and tuck solutions when the fix requires major surgery and direct confrontation. Most common–validating everyone's position without taking a stand, so every sib believes Parent sides with him or her when they don't. Another strategy to smooth ruffled feathers is "the payoff"–Parent gives something valuable to an injured party, so they keep quite and tow the line.

- **The ostrich method:** This requires putting your head so far down in the sand you could wiggle your nose and tickle China. This optimistic Parent hopes that, with time, things will work out. In the meantime, they ignore the problem and keep their fingers crossed.

So, what can Parent do to alleviate the situation? A lot. But ultimately, it's the Sibs that have to do the heavy lifting. Parent can bring the Sibs to the peace table, but only the Sibs can make the peace.

Six Action Steps for the Sibling Rivals

Action Step #1

Admit you're part of the problem, too.

If you're similar to most Sibling Rivals, you're in denial. You think your brother or your sister is the problem. News flash: so are you, because every sib working in a family business cares what Dad thinks of them and how they're doing compared to other family members. And you, being human, have an exquisitely sensitive fairness meter that pops a coil every time it sees a Sib getting more than you think they deserve.

You have to come to grips with your own feelings before you deal with your other sibs. You may not be the instigator of the problem or even its worst offender, but you, like your other sibs, are part of the problem. Gage the severity of your sibling rivalry by taking our Rival for the Title Test. Afterward, we'll show you how this test will be the single most powerful method to bring sibling peace.

The Rival for the Title Test

- ➡ You sometimes discount the recognition a sib receives for doing a good job.
- ➡ You secretly want to say, "I told you so" when a sib goes against your advice and ends up with the problem you warned them about.
- ➡ You're secretly happy to be brought in to fix a problem a sibling caused.
- ➡ You sometimes withhold information that a sib would find useful.
- ➡ You often sit at opposite ends at business meetings or personal gatherings.
- ➡ You get a twinge of jealousy when a sib buys a new car or house.
- ➡ Your sib's family goes out of their way to avoid you at social gatherings.
- ➡ You feel favored because you go to lunch with Parent more than your sibs.
- ➡ Instead of helping a failing sib you sometimes sit back and watch, even if it hurts the company.

Key:

If you answered yes to 1–3 statements: You're part of the problem.

If you answered yes to 4–6 statements: You're a BIG part of the problem.

If you answered yes to 7 or more statements: You're probably the reason the business will be sold or go bankrupt.

Guilty by reason of being human

So you took the test and figured out you can't plead not guilty. Now what? Get your sibs to take the test so you can come to a collective conclusion: "We're all part of the problem." This is critical because without a universal admission there can be no unified solution. You can't fix a problem until everyone acknowledges that there is one.

So, how can you get Sibs to take the test? You can't. Unless all your sibs genuinely look up to you as a leader, they're going to see your attempt as a blame-them-first power grab. They won't answer honestly. Instead they'll accuse you of stirring up trouble. You've got to get the only person who commands power and instills fear in everyone–Parent.

How to get Parent involved: scare him to death. You're not going to surprise Parent with the fact that your sibling rivalries are making things tough both at home and in the office. He has eyes and ears, and a good supply of antacids, we suspect. Remember, the only reason he hasn't done anything about it is because his past attempts failed, he doesn't know what to do, and he figures it'll go away. If you approach him with a plan to end the sib turmoil, he'll be very receptive.

You first have to scare the bejeesus out of him. If you don't, he'll give it a half-hearted try and give up. So here's how you get his fright on: Tell him it's just a matter of time before the sibs bust the business, risk his financial future, and ruin the family legacy. Keep reporting the statistics showing only 10 percent of family businesses survive into the third generation.

If that doesn't put the worry in his wart nothing will. If he agrees to lead the charge, go to Action Step #2. If he'd rather get a consultant or a counselor to do it, then help him pick one out. That would be the best route, because Parent, as we discussed earlier, might be inadvertently contributing to the problems.

Action Step #2

Organize a family "Camp David Summit"

It's time for a family summit–a well-planned meeting to address the sibling rivalry issue and agree on a plan to work together. We're going to assume that Parent is going to lead the charge and that you're going to be backstage guiding him through the process.

Emphasize the importance of the event. Everyone attends. No excuses. Write out the script for Parent if you have to. It should go something like this: "This family isn't working well together. My choices are to sell the business, continue to watch as you destroy what I've built, or do something about it. I've chosen to do something about it. We are going to have one of the most important, high-level discussions this family has ever had. We are going to develop a plan to put us back on track. Attendance is mandatory. The future of the business is at stake."

Pick a place you've never been. It'll signal just how serious the meeting will be. We suggest renting a conference room in a hotel.

Make the test mandatory. Distribute the test to everyone before the meeting with specific instructions: "Answering the questions is mandatory; sharing the answers is not. We'll use the test results as a launching point to develop solutions. We're not going to use this test to play the Blame Game."

Start on a positive note and acknowledge everyone's strength and contribution to the business. Express how lucky everyone is to be a part of the family legacy. Say something to the effect that there's enough room for everyone to be successful, but for that to happen, it's time to think *we*, not *I*.

Bring up the test. This will be one of the most contentious issues because it can so easily lead to unwanted confrontations. We recommend that you start by asking, "By a show of hands, is there anybody in this room that didn't agree with at least one statement in the test?" Social pressure and the risk of ridicule will keep everyone's hands down. If a stray hand goes up, say the same thing you're going to say anyway: "Thank you for your honesty."

Play true confessions. Here, we want you, Sibling, to take the lead. Admit your mistakes and apologize for them. Be specific. For example:

- "Brother, I've criticized you in front of Dad just to make myself look better. I completely understand why that makes you want to pay me back."
- "Sister, I barely congratulated you on your last sale. I'm sure it made you feel that I don't appreciate you or admire what you did."
- "Brother, every time we meet with our managers, I make it seem like a race to see who caught the most fish."
- "Sister, I interrupt you when you have ideas. I'm sure it feels like I don't value your opinion."

It's hard to listen to somebody take responsibility for what they've done and not accept their apology. By publicly owning up to your mistakes, you'll create an opening for everyone else to do the same thing. And once everyone does that, it frees the group to make lasting changes.

Follow our Six Commandments of Conduct. Avoid repeating the same mistakes by setting go-forward rules. Here are just a few we recommend:

1. We will disagree in private. No public assassinations allowed. We will not argue in front of other people. We will resolve issues privately.
2. We will support a group decision even if we individually disagree with it. Dissent is welcome during deliberations, but prohibited after the verdict. We will go forward with one voice after we vote on an issue.
3. We will go through a Sibling Court of Appeals before we take an issue public. When we have a problem with another sibling, we agree to meet as a group to discuss it before going to others in the family or company.
4. We agree our salaries will be based on market for the job. We agree to establish a compensation committee and review our compensation packages each year during our budgeting process.
5. We agree that if we can't fix our problems we will all take a pay cut to hire a senior executive to manage us. We agree that the future of the company is more important than proving who's right or who's more valuable. We agree that, if we can't police ourselves, we will hire someone to do it for us. We agree that Parent will make the decision.
6. We agree to a Company Protection Clause. We will protect the company by requiring all our spouses–no exceptions–to sign prenuptial agreements, so company shares are excluded from marital property. In addition, our shareholders agreement, valuation clauses, buy-out provisions, and estate planning will be reviewed every three years and will not contain evergreen provisions.

The Six Commandments of Conduct are your escape route from disaster. If everyone sticks to it you'll never see that exit approach again. But reality being what it is, chances are that one of the Sibs is going to break all the rules and put the company in danger. Our recommendation: Fire them. Either you let them go or you let them wreak havoc.

Beware of unwarranted optimism. Nothing changes overnight. Old feelings and resentments will linger, no matter how sincerely everyone pledges to change. You're likely to disagree on the way your sister feels about her latest hire, or when the company should open that new office. And if you've been rivals for a long time, expect to cringe when your brother has had a big success. We don't think those feelings will go away, but they will lessen over time. Until they do, here are the best ways to handle those feelings without losing your mind, or bringing your pistol to the office:

- **Grit your teeth and think of the money.** Remind yourself that every individual win contributes to a collective victory. Your brother's new account, your sister's improved customer retention rate, your increased quality control–they all turn into money and they all go into the family business treasury. A little envy is a small price to pay for big profits.
- **There'd be no you without them.** Your business would suffer if you and your sibs thought and behaved exactly alike. The process-oriented, financially inclined, analytical sib who can't see the human side of issues is bound to create a company-destabilizing turnover. But if you have a sib that can balance you out by noting the affect on human resources you might arrive at better decisions. A good manager will want to surround himself with people who have different perspectives, that way he can assess and anticipate the

affect and possible consequences of different options. There are benefits to opposing views. Embrace them; don't push them away.

Action Step #3

Make friends in the foxhole.

After you and your sibs agree on a code of conduct, it's time to get down to business. Imagine you and your sibs on the front lines every day. Make it official–from this day forward, you're going to function as a unit.

Make meeting together routine. Have sibling rivalries kept you from meeting with your brothers and sisters in a business setting? If so, erase the past and set time aside for routine meetings. For those of you working in the day-to-day, once per week is a good start. Begin spending more time together in your business roles with meetings to discuss the latest sales, customer service problems, or employees. This way you'll learn how the others think, how they approach problems, and how they communicate.

The Big Point

If Dad hasn't all ready, make yearly planning and budgeting a formal operating policy. Here are some benefits you'll discover:

1. Forge the sibling alliance. It's your forum to discuss ideas together, make decisions, and face your disagreements.
2. Hold sibs accountable. Put sister on record that she's committed to increasing sales in her store. Make brother account for those high-entertainment expenses he says are business development related.
3. Are you all on the same page? See if there's a match in the vision you and sibs have for the company.

Obviously, you'll meet often with the siblings you work with, but what about the others? Do you have brothers and sisters who don't work in the business but may be owners someday? If so, the others need to be a part of the new sibling unit, as well. Although less frequent, whether once a quarter or every six months to review results and plans, establishing formal meetings will solidify the sibling team.

Play together. You and your sibs must socialize outside the office. No ifs, ands, or buts about it. It's harder to be rude, disrespectful, or disruptive if you have a personal relationship with your co-owners. We're not saying you have to be best friends, but you do need to break bread once in a while. We're not going to go through a laundry list of activities you can do, but there is one secret we want to share with you about becoming friendly: Involve the kids as much as you can. It's an interesting phenomenon–the more cousins like each other, the better their uncles and aunts get along.

Action Step #4

Decide how to decide.

You can't force your sister to agree with you by threatening to pull out her fingernails anymore than you can force your brother to take your side by threatening to slash his tires. You guys have important business problems to resolve. Unless you put some structure around *how* you're going to make decisions, what decisions you make won't matter because your sibs will sabotage it every step of the way until it fails.

If you've been working in the family business for a few years and Parent is moving into the retirement zone, expect interaction with your sibs to be more frequent and intense. What happens when you can't agree on the same direction, the same investment opportunity, the same evaluation of a potential new hire? What happens when you have major disagreements in how to increase sales, lower expenses, and fix customer service problems?

The only way to answer these questions without half the group plotting the other half's death is to, first, decide how you're going to decide.

If Dad or Mom spent most of their career making unilateral decisions, there's no formal mechanism in place when two or more people with differing opinions have to come to a compromise or make a decision. Sibling teams work best when all agree on the way they'll come to a conclusion. Here are some of the best ways to do it:

- **Majority rules.** Select a committee consisting of the sibs, senior managers, and Parent (if they are still in operating mode) to make decisions. We used this method successfully for many years. If, for example, there's an impasse on whether to open a new office, put it to a vote. We suggest you go the Supreme Court route: Always have an odd number of judges so there's no chance of a hung jury. Five on the "Court" seems about right. Nine seems to be a bit much.
- **Consenting Adults.** This is the all-or-nothing approach. Either you reach a consensus or you don't move forward. While trying to please everyone is a nice thought, it's a recipe for paralysis and we don't recommend it.
- **Follow the Leader.** This is the "one person/one vote" method. It only works when the sibs think one of you is capable of making all the operating decisions and the rest are just happy to come to work.

- **Tie-breaking Councils.** When you've reached a serious impasse let your outside advisors break the logjam. You need trusted advisors *who don't work at the company.* If you don't have them, drop everything and assemble one.
- **Mixed Mutt Verdicts.** Mix and match different decision-making methods. You have majority rules on operating decisions and an advisory council on break-the-bank decisions, such as buying out a competitor. You can also put a mechanism in place where a contentious ruling is reviewed at a set time to monitor progress.

Remember, making the right decisions will do you no good if you haven't established *how* you're going to make them. The right business decision that leaves half your sibs resentful will come back to haunt you. The right decision that leaves all the sibs speaking with one voice will not.

Action Step #5

Diffuse the disruptions.

Even with all our suggestions locked tightly in place you still have to deal with the human aspect of life at the office. It's just a matter of time before the sibs get into a fight and one of them says, "I thought he could use a margarita, so I threw it in his face." So, we want to give you a couple of pointers on how to make sure a mini soap opera doesn't balloon into an epic drama. Here are some of the most common problems you're going to encounter and the best way to deal with each:

Problem: My brother wants his wife to work part-time in the business so they can bring home extra cash. I don't like her and don't want her at the company.

Solution: Is it worth the ill feeling you'll have with your sibling by saying no? You'll probably be better off saying, "Look, I don't think having our spouses working in the business is a good idea. But because this has come up, we'll give your wife a part-time position for six months and then reevaluate whether it's working. If I'm uncomfortable, let's agree to help her find another job elsewhere."

Of course, you're better off with guidelines ironed out before this one crops up. Get the group together and start with the big question: Can spouses work in the family business or not? If so, you'll need to determine the credentials they'll need to join. Of course, the most important credential will be left unsaid: Are they well liked by the family or not?

Problem: My sister takes too much time off and goes home early too often.

Solution: This usually boils down to an issue of fairness, commitment, and accountability. If Dad let him or her get away with such behavior, you're probably going to have a rough time getting a course correction. Start some gentle prodding with new rules, such as job descriptions that spell out expected office hours, vacation time, and so on. This alone may solve the problem without any direct confrontation. For sibs that can't read the writing on the wall, you'll need to have a private discussion. If you've taken our suggestion to have weekly meetings, bring it up there. Don't be accusatory. Instead, say, "Gee, I've noticed you're leaving early a lot. Is something going on in your personal life?" If the answer is no, that's your cue to step in with, "We're all here until closing and think you should be as well."

Your biggest problem may be how it looks to the rest of the employees. If they see sib leaving early, they'll wonder why they should bust their butts for the company. Remember, we've stressed that family working in the business should realize they are ambassadors of the company and are held to a higher standard. Let sibling know you are concerned that his or her work habits will affect the employees.

Problem: My sibling has huge travel and entertainment reimbursements that I know aren't business-related.

Solution: This one may be another habit inherited from Dad, who charged everything to the business. Now that the business is supporting more family members, the extras can get out of control. Get your sibs together and a set guideline for travel and entertaining costs so everyone knows their expense account isn't an ATM.

Problem: My brother's wife frequently strolls into the office in her tennis dress with her barking poodle to use the copy machine.

Solution: We understand it is a family business, but you must have a professional code of conduct in the office. Take your brother aside and tell him you overheard some comments from the employees. You think it's best for your sister-in-law to come in after work hours.

Action Step #6

What to do when you just can't seem to work together.

Sometimes nothing works. Sometimes family ties become rubber bands–stretched beyond their ability to bounce back. Sometimes an army of independent directors and mediators won't be able to get you to see eye-to-eye. Whether it was apparent from the beginning or it became intolerable once Parent moved aside, you've reached the end and need to split up. What are your options?

Hire a family business therapist. If you haven't tried this yet, a family therapist may be worth a Hail Mary pass–a last resort attempt to win the game. If your sibs roll their eyes at the suggestion, move on to our next option.

If, on the other hand, you receive a positive response, set out to find the right therapist and give it a go. When you've had reasonable relationships with your sibs in the past, there's a chance a neutral, experienced facilitator could get you to the missing compromise, or revelation, that ends the logjam. Your sister may need to hear you say it was always clear Dad loved you best and she had an uphill struggle in the family. Or, brother wants you to thank him and recognize his big contribution from 20 years ago. If the sibs can climb above their barbwire wall of emotions and see the big picture, they might get a glimpse of a brighter future.

Split the existing business. This is a good option when the business is big enough to divide into parts, letting each sib run one. We did this twice: once with a family member and once with a non-family partner. Whether you divide by geography, product lines, or some other way, at least the family isn't throwing away the economic platform that took years to build. Once you're out of your sibs' hair in day-to-day business operations, hopefully, you all can go back to some degree of family harmony.

Sell your shares to the others (or buy out your sibs). If everyone agrees on this option, the three critical factors are valuation for the shares, payment terms, and collateral for the notes unless the amount is paid in a lump sum. By now, you should have a shareholder's agreement that dictates the procedures. Problems arise when that agreement has unrealistic terms and conditions that put the company at risk. We discussed the basics on shareholders agreements in Chapter 1, but in the sibling era, make sure your agreements are reviewed every three to five years and contain up-to-date valuation methodologies or formulas and terms that don't break your back.

Sell the company to a third party. Often, this is the most emotional outcome for the family. Everybody may leave with a fatter bank account, but nobody escapes the sadness of destroying the family legacy. Still, it may be the best option. Sometimes the sanity of the family is more important than its legacy.

Chapter Summary

The Sibling Rivals

- **Action step #1:** Admit to yourself that you are part of the problem. Express the danger to the business with Parent and help him or her organize a family summit.
- **Action step #2:** Use a family summit to address the problems with the other siblings. Some key points:
  - Make attendance mandatory.
  - Discuss the problem openly.
  - Agree on the Six Commandments of Conduct.

- **Action step #3:** Make friends in the foxhole. You and your sibs need to function as a unit. Make meeting together and socializing a normal routine.
- **Action step #4:** Decide how to decide. We recommend majority rules.
- **Action step #5:** Expect to deal with the human aspect of life at the office with your sibs. Diffuse the disruptions before they derail your partnership.
- **Action step #6:** When you just can't work together consider three options: (1) splitting the business, (2) selling your shares to the other sibs (or buying them out), or (3) selling the company to a third party.

Uncle Ben Marries...Again

"Someday, son, 50% of this will belong to your ex-wife."

Chapter 7

There's only one phrase that can damage a family business more than "I do," and that's, "I want a divorce."

In a family business, when one person goes through a divorce or remarriage, the entire family feels it. The ripple effect is inescapable. Yes, you have the normal battles (custody, child support, and alimony, but not many publicly owned corporations went bankrupt from a messy divorce. Your business could, and that's why we're going to show you how to build a moat around your business to protect it from marauding divorcees, ex-husbands, ex-wives, new in-laws, ex-in-laws, and entitled stepchildren.

Because anyone in the family can get divorced or remarried, we've chosen one character to represent them all: Uncle Ben. And because we can't take everybody's point of view about Uncle Ben's adventures in love, we're addressing the chapter to the person who has the most to lose: Dad.

But whether you're Dad, Mom, Brother, or Sister, you're going to find out how divorce can bring your company to its knees, and, more importantly, how you can prevent it from happening.

Uncle Ben Marries Again: A Typical Scenario

How can we protect the family business from Uncle Ben's adventures in love?

"It looks like Uncle Ben has a new wife," my son told me. Great. Ex-wife number two was so mad at him she attempted to petition the courts to freeze our company's bank accounts. We had forensic accountants squatting in our conference room for weeks searching for the $400,000 she claimed we were hiding for Ben. "Did he find this one in rehab, too?" I asked.

"Worse," he said. "He met her at a single moms meet and greet. She has got two sons that Uncle Ben wants to bring into the business."

I lost it. "What!? Has he gone crazy? His second wife didn't have any kids and look at the torture she put us through. Can you imagine the trauma if Wife number-three's kids work for us and Ben gives her the heave-ho?"

"Which should be..." said my son, flipping through the calendar, "in about 18 months if history is any indication of the future."

"Listen, Dad, I don't think the company can survive another one of Uncle Ben's marital fiascos. Why does he think he can dump his new stepchildren here when they can't find a job anywhere else? I mean, I love Uncle Ben, but this has gotta stop."

He's right. We have got to figure out a way to protect ourselves from Ben's affairs of the heart. But how (he owns half the company)?.

What's Dad Thinking?

Dad may be happy about 20-percent growth rates, increased productivity, and a patent on the next great widget, but he knows he's one ex-wife away from losing it all.

Let's say Uncle Ben's wife files for divorce. After all the name-calling and creative attempts to make each other miserable, what's left? Money. And where is it? In the family business. And how liquid is it? Not very. Do you see where we're going with this? Dad knows a bad settlement might force him to "liquidate" part or all of the company if the divorce court judge considers the business marital property.

Uncle Ben might be a business champ, but he's a marital chump. He doesn't get prenuptials and that's why he keeps putting the family business at risk. Without a prenup, there are no restrictions on what's considered marital property–the assets the two parties will ultimately split. So, the business gets lumped into the pot with the house, bank accounts, and other assets. Once the business becomes the center of a divorce proceeding, it'll cost a fortune just to determine its value.

Dad sees Uncle Ben's divorces the way the Titanic saw icebergs–a cold way to go under. Do the math and you'll see what we mean: Legal fees to represent the company, forensic accountants crawling all over your books, distracted management, burdensome financial settlements, and more. But none compare to this: the threat of using insider information to extract a far greater settlement than you'd ever consider. It's not unusual for family businesses to have secrets that could harm them if they became public. What if Uncle Ben's ex-wife knew some of those secrets and used it to her advantage?

Even if you survive the financial meltdown caused by Uncle Ben's divorces, you still have to contend with the aftershocks. Uncle Ben's ex is probably not going to exit quietly even if she got all the money she wanted. Say she gets custody of the kids–the ones that could be an invaluable asset to the family legacy. If she succeeds in bad-mouthing your side of the family, what are the chances the kids will want to join the business later on? It's not just money that flies out the window after a divorce–it could be the trust and loyalty of future heirs.

The ending of a marriage isn't the only thing that can ruin a business. The creation of second and third ones can, too. Remarriage forces Dad and his top people to face dilemmas that no other business executives do. Consider this. You're desperate for a new operations director and Uncle Ben's new wife has just the qualifications you need. Or, she has bright, capable children from a previous marriage that could easily fill a spot and help the company. You hire them, right? Only if you have enough aspirin to answer some of the obvious questions–such as how the siblings, nieces, nephews, and children from the first marriage are going to feel. Imagine your new brother-in-law is the regional manager of the local bank and the company needs a credit line. Do you want him to see your financial information and ask questions you'd rather answer to a stranger? There are no easy answers to these questions, but better that you ask them before a court answers them for you.

Four Action Steps for Uncle Ben

The likelihood of someone in your family business getting divorced, remarried, or having stepchildren is pretty high. So you need to know how protect the business from romance (or rather, it's failings). You can't prevent Cupid from slinging his arrows left and right, but you can make sure the points aren't poisoned. Learn how by reading the following Action Steps.

Action Step #1

Protect the business before *a family member marries.*

The best way to protect the business from a messy divorce is for the spouse-to-be to sign a prenuptial agreement. In a prenup, a spouse agrees to exclude the business from dividable marital property in case of divorce. Prenups are cheap, common sense, no-brainer solutions, and we'll bet that you don't have a policy that forces family members who work in the business to sign one if they get married. Most family businesses don't. Why? Well, could you possibly find a more sensitive issue? And let's face it, some family members are simply opposed to them because, if not handled properly, discussion of a prenup could literally ruin their relationship.

About the only piece of good news for a business going through its first ugly divorce is that family resistance to prenups melts faster than butter on a hot griddle.

But what if the family hasn't experienced the negative affect a divorce can have on the business? How do you convince them that a prenup should be a pre-condition to working for the family business, and that, if they don't get one, they don't qualify for ownership?

You do it by showing them what can happen when one of them divorces and there *isn't* a prenuptial agreement. You do it by showing them what can happen when the business is at the center of a divorce proceeding. You do it by showing them how a lack of prenups could mean risking their nest eggs. The best way to do that is to have them read this list:

Why Everybody Has to Sign a Prenup

- *Money down the drain:* You'll need to hire a lawyer to represent the company. Expect to double your outside accounting firm's fees for all the questions they'll have to answer from the spouse's lawyer's and accountants. If you can't come to terms, you may be forced to sell the company.
- *Get ready to open your kimono:* The ex will hire forensic accountants to examine your company records. "And by the way," they'll ask, "why didn't you report Uncle Ben's expense account as part of his compensation?"
- *A hostile valuation:* The accountants Uncle Ben's wife hires will value your business higher than yours will. And that guy who wears a black robe to work is going to decide who's right. You had better hope he's never been fired from a family business.

- *A never-ending witchhunt:* Bank accounts can be frozen. Uncle Ben's ex is convinced you're moving money around. Her team is looking for secret accounts and maybe property that Uncle Ben purchased in another family member's name to hide his assets.
- *Depositions for everyone:* Employees in the financial side of your business will be grilled over and over. They'll be asked about Uncle Ben's compensation, his expense accounts, insurance, deferred compensation, and how many bathroom breaks he has on the average day.
- *Meet you new partner:* If you refuse to liquidate any part of the business, you may have to live with the unthinkable: Having Uncle Ben's ex-spouse as your future business partner. Yikes!

If this list doesn't make every working member of your family dive for pens, contracts, and prayers for retroactive prenups, we don't know what will. Bottom line: If you want to protect the business, prenups must be mandatory with absolutely no exceptions. That "no-exceptions" policy will not only protect the business, but ironically, it'll also make it easier for family members to ask their future spouses for a prenup. Read on and you'll see why.

How do you bring up a prenup?

Okay, so you've convinced everyone that prenups can save the business in a divorce proceeding. Everyone understands that, if there's a sneeze in anybody's marriage, the family business gets pneumonia. They've all agreed to make prenups a pre-condition for working in the business. and that if somebody gets married without one they lose his or her stake in the business. But you can't just leave it there. Demanding a "what" without showing them a "how" is unfair, insensitive, and worse, runs the risk that you're going to lose valuable family employees.

For example, how do you convince your totally smitten, romantic daughter, who's a star in the business, that she *must* get her fiance to sign a prenuptial agreement? What if the fiance refuses and she has to choose between the love of her life and the job that she loves? That's why we've come up with a plan that acknowledges the sensitivity of the issue and provides a caring, thoughtful, but firm approach that your family members can use.

1. *Tell stories about Uncle Ben's divorces*

Don't wait until you're in love before you bring up the subject of how divorces almost ruined your family business. There shouldn't be any mention of prenups–just funny and not-so-funny stories about life in the family biz. By introducing the family's near-death experiences with drive-by divorces, you set early expectations that if the relationship gets serious, the family will expect protection from all its members.

2. *Talk early, talk often*

Your first talk about signing a prenup shouldn't be when he's on bended knee asking for your hand, or at the altar. You'll put unfair and undeserved pressure on your relationship. Worse, your future spouse is likely to perceive it as a power play where you corner him or her with a last-minute demand. Your first concrete conversation should take place at the first hint of a future engagement. Talk about it often, so that the conversation is never about whether or not there should be a prenup, but what it should look like.

3. Frame the prenup as a way of protecting your spouse's interest in the business

Don't insult your future spouse's intelligence by saying the prenup is all about protecting *him.* Still, as Henry Kissinger once famously said, "it has the added advantage of being true." Meaning, prenups *do* protect your future spouse–from the failed marriages of other family members.

The truth is, if someone such as Uncle Ben doesn't sign a prenup, it jeopardizes your future spouse's financial well-being. He or she may not be working in the business, but they're tied into it through you. And if your salary/dividends/stock are negatively affected by Uncle Ben's lack of a prenup, your spouse is going to feel the squeeze.

4. Talk about other "policies for spouses" to which the family has collectively agreed

This includes the family's policy on hiring spouses, selling products or services to it and other subjects. This will put the prenup in a more acceptable concept–namely, the family business has "many" rules and the prenup is just one of them.

5. Offer a financial alternative that doesn't include the family business

"Is the family business more important to you than I am?" It's a typical question when love mixes with money, so tread carefully. How you handle this can affect the way your future spouse feels about the family and the business for his or her entire life. Always start with an expression of empathy for your future spouse's concerns about *his or her* financial position if your marriage doesn't work out. *Especially* if he or she decides to stay at home and raise the children. His or her concerns are legitimate, and the more attention you pay to them, the likelier he she will be to sign a prenup.

6. Tell him or her the prenup isn't a personal option, but a family policy

You own a part of the business, not all of it, and as part owner you don't have a choice–a prenup is a condition of ownership.

7. Tell your lawyers it's not about winning.

The right tone in a prenup can make the difference between somebody signing it or dumping you. Lawyers tend to think that representing you is about gaining leverage at any cost. Don't let them. Be sure they understand that the way they conduct the discussions is as important as the outcome.

Action Step #2

Protect the business after *a family member marries.*

So, your super-smart kid, who you're convinced will run the company someday, didn't get his spouse to sign a prenup. Now what? You're in a tight spot; how do you protect the business from one of its future owners? The good news: You have several options. The bad news: they all require lawyers.

- The post-nuptial agreement. Similar to the prenup, same concept, different timing. It's a legal agreement excluding the business from marital property, but it's signed after you're married. It's sort of like closing the barn door after the horse escaped, but can work if you replace that asset with something of similar value.

- ➡ Put the kids' shares in a trust. This is a time-tested and highly successful way of keeping ownership from the reach of a divorce settlement. When you are ready to pass your shares to the kids, call your friendly lawyer to set up a trust that will own the shares. That's right, the kids don't own the shares, the trust does, so the shares are not considered dividable marital property. Of course, you'll have to find someone you trust to act as trustee.
- ➡ Create two classes of stock: voting and nonvoting. Consider creating two classes of stock, voting and nonvoting, and pass the nonvoting share to the kids. The trick here is the nonvoting shares aren't worth as much as the voting shares. The sharks can still come after you, but the bites won't hurt as much with dull teeth.
- ➡ "Restriction on transfer of shares" clause. Most shareholder agreements contain a clause forbidding transfer of shares to third parties without permission from other shareholders. If you don't have this clause, drop this book now and get one. The clause protects the company from the Uncle Bens of the world who believe that love means sharing stock with golddiggers.

Action Step #3

Protect the future management of the family business after the divorce.

It cost the company a bundle, but you survived Uncle Ben's divorce. It's over. Or is it?

Let's say Uncle Ben's ex gets custody of the children and you think they're exceptionally bright. In fact, you think when they grow up they'd be a great addition to the business. Good luck. If Uncle Ben's ex-wife has a grudge that won't budge those children will end up working for your competitor. You see, even though she's not an in-law anymore, Uncle Ben's ex is still a stakeholder in the family business. How so? The kids live with her (or spend half the time with her), which means she is responsible for raising and grooming your family business heirs. Because her defamatory words can slice the family legacy into bite-sized morsels, we're calling her the "Ex-Wife With a Stiletto Knife."

How do you know if Uncle Ben (or anybody in the family) has an Ex-Wife With a Stiletto Knife? When she does everything she can to paint you, your family, and even the business with the "bad" brush. These are the three biggest signs to watch out for:

1. *She's uncooperative when it comes to juggling the visitation schedule with the kids.* Example: You have an important Friday afternoon sales pitch that could double the operations, but it's your weekend with the kids. You need her to switch out the schedule, but she has something much more important than doubling the growth of the business–a tennis match.
2. *She turns up the volume against you and your family.* If the kids are getting a daily dose of "Dad is Bad" that you can't be trusted, you left them, you don't really love them–how will they function in a family business with you in the driver's seat?

3. *She's willing to hurt you and the business even if it means hurting herself and the kids.* Once an ex grabs that knife, everything flies out the window, including rational thinking. Why would somebody damage a business that in part stabilizes his or her financial security or that of the kids? Because Revenge has never been on speaking terms with common sense.

Remember, we're not passing judgment on who did what to whom to warrant the bad feelings. In fact, the ex's anger and thirst for revenge might be totally justified. We're just telling you that knife she's wielding can wind up putting the business in critical care if you don't take precautions. Fortunately, there are things that Uncle Ben and the rest of the family can do to stop the kids from being poisoned by the ex with the hex.

Recruit your family to spend more time with the kids. Assuming Uncle Ben has joint custody or at least reasonable visitation rights, make sure the whole family's involved. It's hard to hate the family business when you love everybody that works in it.

Enlist an army of ambassadors. Recruit the children's grandparents, uncles, aunts, and cousins to be goodwill ambassadors and say great things about you, Uncle Ben, and the rest of the crew. Let them be cheerleaders that offset the negative rap from the ex. Under no conditions should they utter a cross word about the Ex-Wife With the Stiletto Knife. You want to dull the knife, not sharpen it.

Use a family therapist. We're assuming there's no use in bringing Uncle Ben's ex-spouse into a therapy session at this point. On the other hand, a good therapist can help Uncle Ben (or anybody else going through a divorce) heal the pain, hurt, and rifts with the kids. If Uncle Ben is similar to most men, he may not communicate as effectively as he'd like. Using a therapist as an interpreter will help him get his message across.

Show the kids the business. If your children are at least 10 years old, let them connect with the family business by giving them appropriate work for two or three hours on special occasions. Whether it's stuffing envelopes, making copies, or counting office supplies, this exposure will provide a positive experience. Get the most patient person in your office to supervise.

Action Step #4

Be prepared for stepchildren issues in a remarriage.

Remarriage can be a blessing for Uncle Ben, but a curse for everyone else. Children from a second or third marriage, whether they're Uncle Ben's or yours, can rock the boat enough to make everybody sea sick. How do you put stabilizers in for smooth sailing? By addressing some of the most common challenges multiple marriages face in a family business:

Problem #1: The family owning the business doesn't want more "family" working in it.

Let's say Uncle Ben remarries a woman with working-age children. He thinks they are a perfect fit for the family business. The rest of your family doesn't. How do you reconcile the disagreement?

Solution:

Have a proven marriage before you test the stepchildren in the family business. Five years sounds about right. With an

"Uncle Ben" who clearly has a poor track record in marriage, the last thing you need is his stepchildren in the business if wife number three doesn't make it. It will take a frank discussion to remind him of his past and firmly say no. Of course, you can offer to help them find jobs elsewhere.

Problem #2: A potential spouse wants the kids to have the same "equal opportunity" as your kids.

After your engagement, your prospective spouse wants assurances that her children will have the same opportunities for ownership and employment in the family business that children from your first marriage have. You don't think that's fair. What do you do?

Solution:

We think it's overreaching to expect equal treatment so early in the game. If your fiance has also experienced a divorce, he or she should be well aware that not all marriages last forever. So first, explore what's behind the appeal. Is this a way of showing your commitment and love, or a request for financial security? Whatever the answer, tell your fiance, gently that it's best to wait at least a few years to discuss such a commitment.

Your specific situation will dictate how you ultimately resolve the issue. How old are the stepchildren? Will they live with you? We say the younger the children and the longer they live with you, the more likely you'll want to treat them as you treat children from a first family. As an example, if there is no other day-to-day father in the picture and the stepchildren call you Dad, they'll be hurt and confused if you don't. On the other hand, if the children are older, say in their teens or 20s, your feelings may be different. Only time will tell.

Problem #3: The children from your first marriage consider your stepchildren as outsiders and think it's unfair if you treat them equally in the family business.

You feel perfectly at ease with your stepchildren and want to include them in the family business. But you've been forewarned: If you think Sibling Rivalry can bring down a business, wait until you see what step-sibling rivalry can do. How do you handle it?

Solution:

You can't, so don't. Unless you have managed to make the perfect blended family, you're in for a rough ride with mixing children from two marriages in business. As we previously discussed, the younger the children at the time you remarry, the more likely you'll be successful at this almost impossible task. Otherwise, help your stepchildren find jobs elsewhere.

Chapter Summary

My Uncle Ben Marries...Again

The divorce or remarriage of any stockholder in a family business can turn the family business upside down. Follow these steps to protect the business and you'll make the next generation of management work for you, not against you.

- **Action Step #1:** Make Pre-nups a no-exception policy. You can protect the business in other ways–putting the kids' shares in trusts, issuing nonvoting stock, and putting restrictions on stock transfers, but really, you're just rearranging the deck chairs on the Titanic. If you want to avoid the icebergs, you must have a prenup policy with teeth. Meaning, if a member of the family doesn't agree, they lose their opportunity for ownership in the business.

- ➡ **Action Step #2:** Instruct the family how to discuss a prenup with a loved one. Use the "talk early, talk often" approach, explain how the prenup protects your spouse from other family member's failed marriages, and offer an alternative that doesn't include the business.
- ➡ **Action Step #3:** Offset the bad P.R. from your Ex-Wife With the Stiletto Knife. If she's going to mount a public relations campaign against the family, prepare your own offensive to counteract the effect on the kids. Spend quality time with them, enlist an army of goodwill ambassadors (other family members who talk up the family), and get the kids involved in the business early.
- ➡ **Action Step #4:** Consider all of the implications of bringing in stepchildren to the family business. Adding stepchildren to the family business mix can cause more problems than you will be able to solve. Unless you've made the perfect blended family, we say don't attempt it.

The Savvy Sister With the Killer Resume

Chapter 8

"YEAH, THAT USED TO BE MY PLACE—MY SISTER BOUGHT ME OUT."

There's one of you in almost every family business: the brilliant kid with a sharp business mind who never joined the family business. You could be the oldest, the youngest, a son, or a daughter, but we're going to call you the Savvy Sister With The Killer Resume. You, similar to so many others, went off because you wanted to chart your own course or because you didn't want to deal with the family dynamics, the sibling politics, and Dad's need to control everything.

So, you struck it big in the corporate world. You got everything you wanted–a big salary, a great staff, a corner office and the kind of status and prestige reserved for the business elite. But your position has a curse much like the Plotnick diamond we talked about earlier (the curse: Mr. Plotnick came with the diamond). You have several "Mr. Plotnicks," actually: Little time for your children or yourself, a lack of purpose and meaning, and no legacy to bestow.

Suddenly, in the middle of your uncertainty, Dad calls and puts on the kind of charm offensive he reserves for his top clients. He wants you to join the business. Badly. What do you do? Do you stay in the corporate world that pays you well, respects your accomplishments, and gives you the kind of status and prestige that you never dreamed of? Or, do you join the family business where you'll have a smaller staff, less status or prestige, but lots of quality of life benefits?

We can't tell you the answer, but we can certainly tell you how to get to it. We'll review the questions you should ask yourself and the family, how to weigh the pros and cons, and how to break the news of your decision, especially if you decide to stay put.

The Savvy Sister's Dilemma: A Typical Scenario

Should I leave my high-powered job for the family business?

"While you were in conference, your father called about Saturday," my assistant says. "Thanks," I reply, knowing this weekend could be a major turning point in my life. My father wants me to join the family business and for the first time, I'm considering it.

On the one hand, I seem to have everything–a successful career, a wonderful husband, two kids I adore, and enough money to afford the good life. I've been told I'll get the big promotion by the end of this year. That means more money, a great title, and–of course–longer hours.

I'm beginning to feel something is missing. The job is a rat race, and while I'm winning the race, at the end of the day, I'm still a rat. I'm always working, always on call, always stressed out. And for what? If I drop dead tomorrow, what have I left behind–a bunch of pay stubs, and two kids and a husband that didn't get enough of my attention. And my legacy? Ha! An empty office that will be restocked in a matter of days.

After the corporate experience I've had, I'm sure I could run the family business. Certainly, that's what dad has in mind. In the long run, it could give our family a lot more financial security and even provide jobs and ownership for my children. It's sure better than what I'd leave them today.

I discuss the pros and cons with my husband, who's not a big fan of my father. "You think you can work with 'The Dad'?" he begins, and then reminds me why I opted out of joining the family business in the past. "Remember your summer breaks in college? You tried working with him but he was a bull-headed male chauvinist who micro-managed everything you did. Plus, you'd have to deal with your brother and cousin who have been at the company for years. How cooperative do you think they're going to be when you, who's never worked in the family business, waltzes in and becomes their boss? I'm afraid you'd be miserable."

He's right. I had a horrible experience working with Dad when I was younger. Still, Dad's tone is different now. I think he really respects what I've done because he's not just asking me to join the business, but to take it over after he retires. He's been after me for months now and I keep saying I don't know. It isn't fair to Dad to keep him on hold when he could hire a professional manager. This is my last chance to join the family business, but I don't know how to come to a decision.

What's the Savvy Sister Thinking?

The clock's ticking on a decision that will permanently affect her life. If she stays in her current job, she may be passing up the opportunity of a lifetime. If she leaves, she might end up trapped in a family quicksand.

Savvy Sister has a lot to consider. It's not like she's weighing an offer from the competition, where reason and rationality drives the decision. She's weighing an offer that's a cross between an entrepreneurial venture and moving back in with her parents. Emotion might not drive her decision, but it's going to be a hell of a back-seat driver.

Obviously, there are advantages and disadvantages of joining the family business. If Savvy Sister spent years surviving corporate mergers, fighting corporate politics, and racing to out-maneuver the ever-younger colleague or new technology, she probably wants more control of her professional life, not to mention her personal life. After all, she has to put in an awful lot of hours at the office to stay where she is.

A move to the family business gives her the opportunity to act as a principal, making decisions without bosses and colleagues evaluating each move and pouncing at the first mistake. Not to say that family business is always a kinder, gentler place to work, but as part of the family, it puts her at or near the top of the food chain.

A quality-of-life factor entices Sister. Yes, she'd lose status and prestige if she left a big company, but other factors have become more important. It's easier to ask your colleague to cover for you while you take your son to his little league game if that colleague is your brother. Your weekend work won't disrupt your family as much when you can do it with Dad at your house instead of the office. In the end, there's more meaning to the blood, sweat, and tears because of the fulfillment of building a family asset—one that can be passed to your children.

Sounds great. So why isn't the move to the family business easy?

Professionally, Savvy Sister may feel she's taking a step down. If she's risen to the top in a prestigious organization, she enjoys the perks, the intellectual stimulation, the status. Whether it's the car service from work at 7 p.m. every night or the look that says "I'm impressed" when she hands her elegant business card to a new contact, Sister knows it can't be taken for granted. Then, there are the day-to-day work issues if she's going from a large corporate organization to a smaller business—more do-it-yourself than delegating, no department to answer your human resources needs, and the tedious slog back to yesterday's technology.

From a strictly professional view, there are other things to consider before she makes the jump: Does she like the industry her family business is in? Is the company based in a city that she doesn't like? If it's a male-dominated industry, will she have to face the kind of harassment or condescension that her big corporation works hard to eliminate? And what about salary? In many cases, it's highly doubtful that the family business can match what she's earning.

All those questions are important, but they pale to the mother of all questions: "Do I really want to work with my family and take the chance of ruining my relationship with them?"

Four Action Steps for the Savvy Sister

Savvy Sister needs a roadmap to guide her to the right decision. That's why we've designed an assessment tool that considers both her professional and personal needs. No matter what the decision, our Action Steps help Sister get what she wants without injuring the family relationship.

Action Step #1

Make a professional and personal assessment.

Our professional and personal assessment will gauge where you are in your career and whether working for the family is a good move. We want you to analyze your current job satisfaction separately from any concerns about working with family. So, we've divided the assessment into two parts.

Take your professional temperature. First, review these questions to pinpoint how you feel about your current job:

- Do you like your job?
- Is your work challenging?
- Are you happy with your compensation package? And the perks?
- Do you have a good relationship with your boss? Your customers? Your staff?
- Does the job give you the fulfillment and purpose you want?

- Do you have enough personal time?
- If you have kids, does your job allow you to spend enough time with them?
- Do you have a real shot at joining the "C-suites?" (CEO, CIO, COO, and so on).
- Is your family's offer the only career change you'd consider?

If you've answered yes to most of these questions we think you should stay put in your current job (unless there's a health crisis in the family). Why leave a job with which you're satisfied for a job that might turn out to be a professional and family problem? You can take the next part of the assessment, but you might want go directly to Action Step #4 and learn how to say no gracefully.

If you answered no or maybe to most of these questions then it sounds as though you'd consider a move, but is the family business the right place to park yourself? Let's find out.

Take your family temperature. We think it's your biggest consideration. Will you enjoy working with your family? Answer these questions to determine your family temperature:

- Have you ever worked for your family's business? If so, did you like it?
- Do you have a good relationship with family members that work in the business?
- Does the family respect you for your career accomplishments?
- Can you be happy reporting to a family member? Will family members be happy reporting to you?
- Does the family resolve issues in a healthy way?
- Will working with family bring you closer together?
- Do you like where the office is located?

- Are your husband and kids (if any) positive about a move to the family business?
- Will working for the family make you wealthier?
- Will working for the family give you personal time?
- Do you have specific skills or experiences that your family business needs?
- Will you be taking an executive position? Is there a real shot to run a division or become president?

If you've answered yes to most of these questions it sounds as though making the move is the right thing to do. Now, let's combine the results of the two assessments and come up with a pros and cons list. It should look something similar to the following chart, only with a lot more input from you.

Should I Stay or Should I Go?

Pros	Cons	Considerations
I'll be my own boss. No more marching to someone else's drum.	Dad's a control freak and I know he'll be looking over my shoulder. Plus, we have two completely different management styles.	Is Dad retiring soon? Has he asked you to be his successor? Short-term pain might make for long-term gain. It all depends on how difficult Dad will be to work with.
I love the idea of ownership in the family business and building its value. It is security for the future.	I'll have more wealth at retirement, but I'll take a cut in salary today. Will my family resent me for lowering their standard of living?	Can you increase the value of the business? The business is not where it should be; that's why Dad wants you to join. You have the smarts, but do you have the stomach?

Pros	Cons	Considerations
I'll have much more control of my personal life and will spend more time with my family.	"Family" may jump in size to include my sister, brother, sister-in-law, and parents.	Are closer relationships with your family a good thing or a bad thing? If you have small children it will be great—instant babysitters and lots of support. If you have a rocky relationship with some of your family members, then it might not be such a good idea.
Calling the shots in my family's business might be better than any promotion I could get from my company.	I'm a shoe-in for partner next year. I'll never be able to make that kind of money in my family's business—not for a few years, anyway.	Some risks are courageous; others just plain stupid. A good financial analysis of the business would go a long way toward determining what kind of risk you'd be taking.

Action Step #2

Get all of the important facts.

At this stage of your analysis, we're going to assume that you want in or are seriously considering it. As with any job offer, never agree to anything without a little detective work. Focus on three areas: (1) analysis of the company, (2) research on the industry, and (3) spying on the family. Did we say spying? We meant poking around and turning over a few rocks. The following are a few recommendations on how to play detective.

Dig deep. Assuming Dad is making the offer, tell him you'd like the company's financial statements and any industry-related information. If the company is a member of an industry trade association, ask Dad if you can contact them, using the company's name, to learn about the competition, trends, new technology, and any other useful information.

You are looking for anything that causes concern: a dip in sales volume, a downward trend in the industry's margins, or a need for major investment in technology. It's not that Dad is hiding anything, but it's best not to be surprised a month after you've joined the company that they are about to lose their biggest customer or a special process Dad pioneered is no longer special.

You need at least two meetings to get your facts straight and discuss anything about the offer that leaves you uncertain. Don't kid yourself about your talks with Dad. They're interviews, not meetings. And *you're* doing the interviewing. Keep it informal, but with a professional air. Your tone should be warm, inquisitive, and positive, but unmistakably professional. You have to make a decision independent of your love for the family; keeping a certain distance will help.

Always phrase your questions positively. Let's say you've learned the best performers in the industry have made significant investments in technology, but the family business hasn't. Asking why is legitimate. Asking rudely is not. Don't question his judgment, question his strategy; for example: "It seems three of your competitors have made investments in technology that are going to significantly speed up their delivery time. What's your plan to compete with that?"

Ask the hard questions. Can you imagine asking the president of a Fortune 500 if he has a slacker son on the payroll? Of course not! You'd be shown the door. But you're going to have to ask those types of questions because family dynamics will play a major role in your decision. The following are just a few questions you should ask.

Where do I fit in the organization chart?

Will I report to a family member? Who? Does a family member report to me? An organization chart in a family business can be convoluted and confusing, having family members and long-term employees with meaningless titles or even "no show" jobs. If you'll be reporting to someone other than the family member making you the offer, spend time with them, making sure you're clear on their responsibilities and yours.

Obviously, if you have friction with anyone you report to or with anyone who'll be reporting to you, you'll want to discuss it further or consider if the family business is a good move.

Who is the ultimate decision-maker?

Figure out who has the power in the family business. If it's Dad with 100-percent control, you'd better make sure you see eye-to-eye on everything. Question him about business strategy, his long-term managers that never say no to him, and his vision of your working relationship.

Who influences the decision-maker?

This is actually a question for other family members, though it pertains to Dad. Dad may rule with an iron fist, but is there a cousin or brother who plays the role of consigliore to Dad?

What happens when family members disagree?

Once you know how power is distributed, ask what happens when there are disagreements among family members. If a mechanism is in place to resolve disputes, be sure you understand exactly how it works and ask for examples of how disputes were resolved. Is there an outside board? An advisory council that breaks an impasse? The last thing you want is to have a major disagreement with a family member and not have a process for resolution.

What's the plan for succession and transfer of shares?

We're assuming you'll be joining at a senior level, so you have the right and obligation to ask this. If you want to own shares, you'll need to learn about Dad's plans. Ask about the capital structure of the company–the classes of stock, how voting rights are distributed, who holds stock, and how shares are held (outright, in trust, and so on). He should be willing to divulge his estate plans as well. Review any shareholder's agreement, bylaws, work agreements involving family or long-term employees, and trust agreements.

When will Dad retire?

If he hems and haws, mumbling that he hasn't thought about it, gently press him. Try to coax him into a discussion that gets you what you need to know. Is he a Father With Farewell Paranoia who has the normal change of life pangs, or is he a "die at the desk" type? Is he expecting the business to continue to pay him after he's working less or does he have a financial nest egg outside of the business?

How does my compensation package compare with others in the family?

If you are not in a family business, you may think this is a nosy question. After all, how can you ask what others make at the company, right? Wrong. Family members *do* find out what the others are making, and if there are significant differences when responsibilities are similar, there will be problems. So ask, and, if there are great disparities, ask why and what compensation policies can be put in place to match the pay scale to the skill set.

Action Step #3

Getting to yes.

Okay, you've gotten the minor details worked out and most of the major ones, but maybe you've hit the wall with one or two deal breakers. If it's business and not family-related, ask to meet with the company's accountants, lawyers, board, or even a customer or two. If you don't like specific aspects of the job then get back to Dad with your own proposal. Whatever the situation, give him the date on which your decision will be made.

So, let's say there are a couple of worrisome aspects about taking his offer. What do you do? The same thing you do with any job offer–negotiate. Here's how:

Be clear about the obstacles

Don't make vague statements such as, "Something doesn't feel right, but I don't know what." Be specific.

- **Reporting structure.** You can suggest something such as, "I don't feel comfortable reporting to my brother; I'd rather report to you." If Dad wants you bad enough he'll change the reporting structure.
- **Money.** Most people move to a new job to make more money and face more challenges. If Dad's offering you a cut in pay, bring in your pay stub and ask how "we" can close the gap. There's nothing like seeing numbers in black and white to bring home the discrepancy. However, if he promises ownership, or a shorter workweek with a vast upgrade in your quality of life, then rethink the pay cut. Remember, nobody on his or her deathbed says, "I should have made more money." But they often say, "I should have spent more time with my family."
- **Ownership.** If Dad is asking you to leave your high-profile job, you're not out of line asking for ownership or a commitment in the company. Ask him if he has already made commitments to other family members.
- **"No grudge" clause.** You say, "I think my brother will have a problem working for me." Dad says, "Don't worry, I take care of it." You're skeptical, but most concerned that a bad outcome will stain your relationship with Dad. Tell him you want a "no grudge" clause if your worst fears come true.

Stand up when you're sitting on the fence

You have the best and final offer from Dad. All your questions are answered yet you're still stuck on maybe. What's next? Flipping a coin? Rock or scissors? A fortune teller? No. A jump. We land on the side of the family business. After all, the decision isn't irrevocable. Give it a year and see what happens. In life, the only thing worse than regretting something you did is regretting something you didn't do. So, if you're sitting on the fence with "analysis paralysis," allow us to give you a gentle push.

You can thank us later.

Action Step #4

Say no to the job without saying no to your family.

So, you weighed the pros and cons, you did the due diligence and, for whatever reason, you've decided to stay where you are. How do you say no without generating bad feelings? You are concerned about the fallout from delivering the news—you don't want this to be seen as a rejection of the family.

For simplicity, we'll assume you need to deliver the news to Dad. You have a difficult mission: Don't hurt his feelings, don't make him angry, don't injure your relationship. A friendly e-mail isn't going to do the job. Neither will a voice-mail message.

Set the tone

You'll need to pay Dad respect and set up a face-to-face meeting. Let him choose the location. Act like a humble guest, show sincere appreciation for his consideration, and stress the importance of family to you.

Explain how you got to no

Tell him how tough it was to come to your conclusion–that you considered the offer, discussed it with your husband, but need to respectfully decline. Here's the important point–the reason you give him doesn't matter as much as the way you say it and the impression he leaves with. For example, don't tell him you anticipated unbearable tension from working with him or others, even if that's the truth. Instead, tell him how important an uncomplicated, loving relationship with family is to you.

If your reasons were financial, tell him you'd love to help in an advisory role, but you need to stay where you are for the family's financial security. If you have the skills that can help the family business, why wouldn't you? It's in your interest to have Dad and family do well financially. Take a few vacation days or weekends from the corporate meat grinder for meetings at the company. Besides, who knows what the future holds? Keep close to the family business so you can step in when you want to–or have to.

Leave the door open, or at least cracked

Unless he's said this is your last opportunity to join the family business, tell him you'd like to reconsider in the future. Either way, thank him and be emphatic that you don't want to injure your relationship.

Chapter Summary

The Savvy Sister With the Killer Resume

Here's a summary of our four Action Steps to help Savvy Sister determine whether to leave her corporate job for the family business. Take these steps to make the right decision:

- **Action Step #1:** Take our two-part assessment and determine whether you are ready to make a professional change, If so, if the family business is the answer.
- **Action Step #2:** Get the important facts to make the decision. Review the company's financial statements and industry-related information. Meet with your family and ask the tough questions.
- **Action Step #3:** If you want to get to yes, don't be afraid to negotiate the items that are deal-breakers for you. If you are still at maybe, we say come down on the side of joining the family business.
- **Action Step #4:** When your decision is no, make sure the family understands that you are rejecting the job, and not them.

The Parent in a Pickle

chapter 9

"Meet the boss's son. The go-to guy whenever you need a piece of string or just a friendly wave."

Dad's dreams of Junior becoming the next CEO are fading fast. Once thought to be a chip off the old block, Dad now questions if he was switched at birth. Worse, the employees at the company already know what has taken Dad time to discover–Junior needs to go.

Dad is heartbroken. He never thought his seat in the boss's chair could be so devastating. How does the parent tell a child, or close family member, that working in the family business isn't working out? Won't it change their relationship forever? What parent wants to take the chance?

We wrote this chapter for the parent who doesn't want to harm a treasured relationship, but needs to deliver some bad news. We'll show you how to pinpoint the issues behind performance problems and suggest ways to get your child's career back on track. If they still keep failing, we'll show you how to compassionately "release" your son or daughter from the company, repair the damage to the relationship, and keep your family together. Finally, for those who want to avoid being the Parent in a Pickle, we have a few pointers.

The Parent in a Pickle's Dilemma: A Typical Scenario

How do I tell my son he's not doing the job without wrecking our relationship?

My son has had four positions in four years. We had to move him from customer service because he kept asking our manager out on a date. We had to remove him from the repair shop because he kept making massive reordering mistakes and now I've gotta take him out of the warehouse because he just wrecked our third forklift.

I can tell the employees have no use for him. When he passes in the hall, they shoot an uncomfortable glance and keep their heads down. I overheard our receptionist joking that the title on his new business card should be changed from "vice president of sales" to "vice president who fails."

That's my son they're talking about! I have to do something, but what? Should I even consider asking him to leave?

My wife lost her mind with that thought: "Leave the company? You can't do that, he's our son!" she said. "You've got to train him, give him some more time," she continues after I give her the recap of his four-year career. "Besides, we have a family business. We should provide our kids with jobs without judging their performance so harshly. I think of it as a safety net for the family."

Oh, right! The family business won't exist if I let him continue on this path. She doesn't have to put up with the business disruptions he causes and what it does to employee morale.

If I don't fix this now, what will happen when my other kids join the business? What would my employees think? I sure wouldn't let them get away with my son's results. I have to do the right thing for the business, but I can't destroy my relationship with my son. What can I do?

What's the Parent in a Pickle Thinking?

It's not working. Your child is floundering in the family business, causing problems wherever he or she goes. Your employees are giving you the "what are you going to do about it?" look every time they screw up. You have to take action, but you're afraid of the effect on one of the most important relationships in your life. Even if you have a human resources department, you can't turn this over to them on Friday and enjoy the family barbeque on Sunday.

It's heartbreaking to face the failure of a child in a family business. Shame, embarrassment, pity, guilt, and anger swirl in a toxic cocktail, finished of course, with a slice of shock. The strong mix of emotions leads to typical, yet highly ineffective ways, of dealing with the problem:

- Deny, deny, deny. Problem? What problem? This Parent simply refuses to face reality thinking, "It's a family business and the kid stays in whatever position I want him in." This one's the easiest on Parent's soul and the hardest on everyone else, including Junior, the business, and the rest of the family. You can only live in the Isle of Denial for so long before reality knocks on the door and wants you to sign for the box of ugly facts he's delivering.
- "Give him time." This is the typical response when Parent recognizes the problem, but makes excuses for it anyway. The big trick is recognizing when time's on your side and when it isn't. An occasional fumble is excusable. Bombing out in three positions in three years isn't.
- Move him around. Here, parent clumsily attempts to solve the problem by moving their son or daughter from department to department, to a different office, or new territory. It's like moving a wrecking ball to see where it can do the least damage.
- Torture the kid. This is the "tough love" approach. Think Marine Corps. Parent decides the only way to get Junior to perform is to humiliate him every chance he gets. Employees try to duck out of any meeting where the two are present.

It's easy to see why Parent takes the easy way out–no confrontation necessary, no time away from more pressing matters. But, there's something else keeping Parent from doing the right thing. The Parent in a Pickle is afraid of being second-guessed by the rest of the family. Parent isn't just risking his relationship with the failing kid, but with everybody in the family who loves him. By now, certain family members are hinting about the ramifications of letting Junior go. It's usually left unsaid, but it always feels uneasy: "We'll blame you if Junior's life gets turned upside down." Visions of Junior and other family members never speaking to him again cloud Parent's judgment.

We've seen similar situations and can guide you to the best outcome. Read our recommendations, remembering to focus on the future, not this moment. As you read them, ask yourself, "What will happen in five years if I do nothing? How will it affect the business? My family?" Our Action steps are designed with this goal: Move Junior out of your business, but not out of your life.

Four Action Steps for the Parent in a Pickle

Action Step #1

Find out why they're failing.

Just because your kid is failing doesn't mean he's a failure. It could be he doesn't have a desire to work for the company, or that he simply doesn't have the skills to do the job you've assigned him. That's why we've designed an assessment tool to discover the cause of the failure.

We've divided the questions into three broad areas–motivation, behavior, and business smarts. Answer honestly and you will move down the path to your ultimate goal: finding a solution that protects the business as well as your relationship with your child.

Motivation

- Did he dream of being something else?
- Can you sense a "what for?" attitude whenever you discuss how sacrifice will benefit the business?
- Is it obvious she is bored with her job, disengaged in meetings?
- Is he on the phone with his friends all day?
- Is "work ethic" missing from her vocabulary?

Your Assessment	Explanations	Solutions
Low motivation in the family business, but passionate about another business.	He never wanted to join the business but he didn't want to disappoint you. Or you unwittingly pressured him into joining the company.	Support his choices and give him your blessing. If he enjoys business, chances are he will come back one day.
No motivation, but passionate about other careers.	She doesn't want to be in business, period.	Give her more education in her area of interest.
Low motivation, seems lost.	He has no idea what he want to do in life, so he has picked your business to be the holding tank until he does.	Life experience can do more than any school or company. You could try: 1. The military. 2. The Peace Corps or related volunteer organization.

Behavior

- How does your child relate to peers, bosses, or clients?
- Is she more interested in her social life than the job?
- Is there an alcohol or drug problem?
- Does he communicate in an aggressive or hostile way?
- Are you worried about a sexual harassment suit because of personal relationships at the office?

Your Assessment	Explanations	Solutions
Bad attitude, worse behavior.	That awful entitlement mentality.	You can give warnings and disciplinary action, but overall it may be best just to fire him or her.
He is bad, but you're not convinced his issues can't be fixed.	Restlessness, boredom, immaturity.	Give him more challenging tasks and measure his progress. He may be sick of their beginner role; suggest more training for a higher position. Maturity issues: They tend to recede with a combination of time and action.

Your Assessment	Explanations	Solutions
She never used to be that way; you sense something is going on in her personal life.	Stress or diagnosable mental health issues such as depression or anxiety disorder.	Do an "intervention" if you suspect drug or alcohol addiction. Encourage her to see a doctor for other issues. We've seen employees turn into good workers after some therapy.
You're baffled because he is high on motivation and he's got business smarts, so why the poor performance?	Some people are simply too embarrassed to admit they don't have the needed skills so they cover up their lack of knowledge with bluster and bullying.	Time for a discussion to determine if a mismatch of skill and job requirements exists.

Business Smarts

- Does she lack the complete understanding of the business?
- Does he take a long time to catch on?
- Is her thinking disorganized and illogical?
- Does he lack the respect of his peers?

- Are you frequently embarrassed because she presents herself poorly or doesn't communicate well in meetings?

Your Assessment	Explanations	Solutions
She's just got no business smarts and no amount of training that is going to change that.	She shouldn't be the captain of the ship, but she can still contribute to the boat.	Keep her at low-level jobs where she can perform and be comfortable.
He's got no business smarts, but he does have people skills.	He may be too afraid of telling you he'd rather be in a more people-oriented department.	Put them in customer service or human resources.
She's pretty smart, actually, but she's lacking skills.	It could be that she feels foolish asking for training, preferring to stumble along, rather than admit that she doesn't know how to do things. Or, worse, she thinks she doesn't need training.	There are management courses and skill-building programs she can attend. Also, she can work for someone else to develop skills and become an accountable employee. If she (or you) think a second chance at joining the family business is warranted, then have at it.

The Big Point

Get Help From People in the Know

The number of local universities and business schools offering courses in family business is exploding. Even the top international MBA programs recognize the vital importance of this segment of the economy. This could be a solution for your motivated child needing more business skills.

Action Step #2

How to tell your child that its not workingout.

You've made your assessment. You've talked it over with close friends, family, and advisors and came up with a plan or at least talking points from Action Step #1. Now, it's time for the moment you've been dreading: The Talk.

Concentrate on your child's welfare. Unless you're dealing with an entitlement attitude, don't frame the conversation about what's best for the business. This is an opportunity to get your child's life back on track, to help them pave a path to their own passions, and ease the difficulty they're dealing with. Stick to that and you'll minimize the damage. Stick to how they're ruining the business and you'll maximize it. Because we've had to go through this ourselves, we have a few suggestions:

Location, location, location

Pick a neutral location–an off-site, quiet place. Better yet, take a walk in the park. It's easier to take bad news in a peaceful, pastoral setting and it sets the tone you want: personal not professional. Here's where not to have the conversation:

Never talk about a problem where it occurs, such as the office. You almost guarantee a negative emotional reaction, setting the stage for a public display that embarrasses everyone. The gossip alone will reach epic proportions. Everybody will give their version of the execution and the first ones who'll hear it will be your clients and vendors.

No way, no how, no homes. Pick your house and you might as well buy stain and odor removers by the case. Your kid will always see your house as tainted–the place where you did the evil deed. Do it in your child's house and you'll both always remember that this is the place you had the "talk that changed everything."

Begin by confirming your love. You only want the best for her. Say something such as, "I love you and want your happiness, but I think that staying at the company isn't accomplishing what we intended. It's putting too much strain on our relationship, and I value that more than anything else. That's why I want to talk to you and see if we can't come up with a resolution we'll both be happy with."

Make it his idea (or at least get their buy-in). This only works if the culprits are low motivation because he doesn't want to be in your company or any business. Start out by saying, "I get the feeling that you'd rather be doing something else somewhere else. If that's true, let me help you do that."

If you can't make it their idea, make it yours. Sometimes you just have to pull rank. But pull it gently. Limit the conversation to how to fix it not what or why. For heaven's sake, don't relive each episode and eruption. That's like talking peace while lacing up the boxing gloves.

Let her leave with honor. If she's still insistent that things can work out, remind her that the decision's been made, but the exit strategy has not. And you want her to decide how that's going to happen. Suggest that she pull the trigger. That way instead of leaving with her tail between her legs, she can exit with her head held high. The more you can avoid embarrassing, shaming, or humiliating her, the more likely you'll preserve the relationship.

Ask them how they want to spread the news. Once you agree on a plan, you'll need to tell the story in a way that's least harmful to everyone. The last thing you want is to cause any more pain and discomfort. Best case scenario: Your child announces his plan. If he refuses, then you announce the departure in the most compassionate way possible: "He's off to pursue his real passion in teaching," or, "he's going to take some well-deserved time off and figure out what he wants to do next."

Action Step #3

Repair the damage and keep your relationship.

After you've delivered the news don't walk away from your meeting with a "business as usual" attitude, or you'll get the relationship you have with other ex-employees. None.

Start turning on the "family" component immediately. Here's our list for effective damage control:

Increase you visibility by pouring on the telephone calls, e-mails, and visits. Expect their response to fall short of what you'd like, but don't be deterred from the effort. Can you do any favors for them that reinforce how much you care? Make calls to help with a job search or arrange lunch with a powerful friend who shares your child's new career interest. The point: Be helpful.

The Big Point

Don't Fear Saying You Are Sorry

Don't think of an apology as something that erases your child's responsibility in the matter. You are apologizing for the fact that your child experienced a painful event.

Turn off the criticism. If you have a habit of making negative comments on anything from where he lives to how he dresses, stop it. Don't even think of reviewing the factoids that led to his departure from the company. You'll risk placing yourself in the "I can't do anything to please my Parent" category, and marginalize everything that comes out of your mouth.

Try to be supportive. This is not the time to nit pick her decision to study poetry. Your child needs to restore her confidence and put "positive" back into her life. Your attitude should be "give it a try," not "are you out of your mind?"

Use money as a salve. You don't want taking your child out of the business to cause a financial earthquake in his life. Depending on the facts you identified in the assessment, you should help financially as much as you can. Say your son's a good guy but not cut out for the business. If he tried, in good faith, to make a go of it, consider an add-on to the company severance that softens concerns about security. For example, if Son is owed three months salary from the company, pony up an additional three to five months or more out of your bank account while they resettle. On the other hand, we don't recommend any cash reward when bad behavior is the reason for the dismissal.

Enlist the family pit crew and make sure other family members are aware of the situation and follow the steps we've outlined. If one family member is closest to the person, ask them to pay special attention in the next few weeks and use a tender heart.

Action Step #4

Avoid being the Parent in a Pickle.

No one aspires to be the Parent in a Pickle. For those of you who want to make sure you're never in the position, we have some suggestions:

- Don't make the family business the inevitable choice. Resist the temptation to push your child into the family business. Yes, adding those two words to your logo–and Sons–may be your dream, but let them have theirs. Sons and daughters who make the choice to join you without pressure will make great workers and extend your legacy.
- Don't let them join you until they've worked somewhere else. We're big on this. Let someone else be their first boss. By the time they join you, they'll understand what's expected in the workplace.
- Don't pay your family "easy money." You may think you're doing them a big favor, but in reality you're putting a golden shackle on them. Once it's on, it'll be next to impossible to get them to willingly move where you want them to go: out the door.
- Don't gamble that working together will make your relationship. If you think that working with your long-lost daughter will give you a chance to become closer, don't bet on it. You need a strong relationship, outside of the family business, before you dive into those uncharted waters.

Remember, family businesses work best when the family in them enjoys each other.

- Don't let one bad apple spoil the whole bunch. If one child (or niece or nephew) always causes problems in the family, don't let him or her join the family business–unless you want to continue the disruptions at the office, too.

Chapter Summary

The Parent in a Pickle

- **Action Step #1:** Find out why they're failing. Determine whether it's motivation, behavior, or business smarts. Finding the cause will help you and him or her move to a solution.
- **Action Step #2:** How you tell your family member it's not working will set the course of your future relationship. Focus on the solutions and leave him or her with honor.
- **Action Step #3:** Repair the damage and keep your relationship. We suggest these key points:
    - Increase your visibility with telephone calls, visits, and e-mails.
    - Turn off the criticism.
    - Be supportive of their future plans.
    - Use money as a salve.
    - Enlist the family pit crew.

- **Action Step #4:** Avoid being the parent in a pickle with the following:
  - Don't make the family business the inevitable choice.
  - Don't let them join until they've worked somewhere else.
  - Don't pay your family easy money.
  - Don't gamble that working together will make your relationship.
  - Don't let one bad apple spoil the whole bunch.

Mr. and Mrs. Inc.

There are few chairs in heaven waiting for the business partners who died loving each other. That doesn't mean you shouldn't go into business with your spouse; but it does mean you better keep the chances of success in mind. When a husband and wife work together, often considered marital suicide, they experience the kind of highs and lows that can even impress the folks at Six Flags.

Mr. and Mrs. Inc. probably began their careers apart, but for many reasons decided that working together would offer a better life–flexible hours, more time with the kids, being their own boss, and building a cash cow that would make the neighbors moo.

Chapter 10

Oh, if it were only that simple. If we sound a little precautionary, it's because we are. We've seen what working together can do to a marriage and what a marriage can do to a business. As with anything, it *can* be done, but you better put in place an unbreakable set of protocols. The principal problem with Mr. and Mrs. Inc. is that the "I do" in the marriage can turn into "I won't" in the business. The potential for conflict escalates exponentially and poses real danger to your relationship. Your main challenge is simple: Can you grow a business without shrinking the marriage?

The answer is yes, if you follow some tried and true advice. We've got a few ideas to make your collaboration successful and prepare you for the inevitable bumps along the way. As in the other chapters, we'll give you practical advice from our own personal experience. We, too, work together as Mr. and Mrs. Inc. and know the potholes, pitfalls, and waterfalls that await you. So, whether you're working together or thinking about it, we've got some business-growing, marriage-saving insights and action items to help you succeed.

Mr. and Mrs. Inc.: A Typical Scenario

Can my spouse and I work together without sinking our marriage?

Geez, if my husband makes one more negative comment about the way I bill customers, I'll kill him! I've got to get out of this office for lunch. Or is this home? Well, actually, it's both. My husband and I share a home office.

Everyone told me I was crazy to work with my husband four months ago, but I didn't listen. It seemed like such a great idea at the time. He was burned out from the corporate rat race and I needed the help. My business was booming, but I was drowning at work. There weren't enough hours in the day to be a businesswoman, mom, wife, housekeeper, and part-time parent to my parents. Oh yes, and lover, too. My balancing act was getting poor reviews. My husband was exactly what the doctor ordered: a smart, experienced man with the skills I didn't have.

He's great with customers and brimming with terrific ideas, but I never imagined that sharing a 15-by-15-feet office could be so bad. Working out of the house had been good for me. Now we're too close for comfort. Does he need his hearing checked? He's so loud on the phone, I can't concentrate. And the Diet Coke cans all over his desk! Good recordkeeping was never my strongpoint, so he has to ask me everything. Every 10 minutes he's interrupting me with, "Where's the customer file?" or, "Did you pay them last month?" Then, there's the inevitable snicker or comment under his breath as he spins his chair away from me!

If the workday isn't bad enough, the evening is worse. After dinner, he still heads for the TV room just as he did when he was a corporate road warrior. There's just one problem—he's not the breadwinner anymore and yet I continue to handle the house, shopping, driving the kids around, and helping with their homework.

Last night, we were close to the breaking point. We had dinner at a great restaurant, and, in passing, I said something about a customer meeting next week. He blasted me, "Why can't we have a romantic evening—remember what that is? Can't you give the business a break? We haven't been husband and wife in weeks and I miss you."

That's his code for sex. Well, how can I want sex at night when he irritates me all day? And never mind him, I'm under so much stress, who can think about sex?

I want to make this work, but I don't know how. My husband is good for the business, but is the business good for our marriage?

What Are Mr. and Mrs. Inc. Thinking?

Mr. & Mrs. Inc. thought they'd become the dynamic duo but they've become Siamese twins instead–joined in the oddest places and unable to go in any direction without dragging or being dragged. They're not used to spending so much time together and the characteristics that might have been mildly annoying are now unbearably obnoxious. Everything's changed. They used to drive to work; now they walk. They used to say, "How was your day, dear?" Now they already know. They used to say "Honey, I'm home," and now they say "Honey, I'm outta here."

What happened? It wasn't supposed to be that way. They both had the same noble motivations. Fed up with the corporate world or other jobs, they wanted something more out of life. The call was powerful–control, purpose, flexibility. The call became a primal scream when they had children, causing work schedules and family life to collide daily. Rushing for the daycare center before it closed, too exhausted to review the homework, out of town for the school play or ballgame–those were just some of the everyday occurrences before Mom and Dad chose to become Mr. and Mrs. Inc.

For other couples, early or forced retirement may have sparked the entrepreneurial bug. With no children (or adult kids) and a seasoned marriage, working together is a dream, not a nightmare. They know they can count on each other, and the partnership just adds more dimension to an already great marriage.

Overall, most couples chance working together for legitimate reasons. It's the execution of the plan that goes astray. So, what goes wrong?

First, there's the transition from the previous corporate environment. When the old days were structured and filled with more people, the change to a smaller organization or even home office makes you feel a little lost and alienated from the outside world. You might miss the stimulation of a daily routine involving different people, projects, and ideas. And, the worst part of course, is doing the things you used to have subordinates do for you. Take for example, a simple thing such as sending an overnight package to a client. What used to take 5 seconds (you simply told somebody to do it) now takes 20 minutes because not only do *you* have to find the materials, pack it, and address it, *you* also have to drive it to the drop-off.

We're often shocked at how naive couples can be about working together. Why does the wife who thinks her husband's closet is a rat's nest believe that his office space is going to be any different? The only thing different is that now she's going to be twice as irritated.

Why does the husband, who knows his wife is terrible at math, suddenly think she'll take care of the books? She won't. Worse, if she has that responsibility, you'll just add to the work-related tension.

So, given all the problems, why do it? Because if you do it right you'll get all the goodies: More time with the kids, more money, a shared purpose, and complete autonomy. The trick is getting it right. Let's start by making sure you're compatible enough to work together and survive the disappearance of what you used to have plenty of: personal space. Then, let's move on to creating a structure for your working relationship, and finally, how to keep the professional side of your relationship from ruining the personal side.

Four Actions Steps for Mr. and Mrs. Inc.

Action Step #1

How to tell if Mr. and Mrs. should be Inc'd.

Never mind what kind of business you want to get into or what experience you bring to it. They mean nothing unless you can answer yes to the following questions:

1. **Have you been married for at least five years?** The first year you're on a perpetual honeymoon. The second year you settle into a comfortable routine. The third year you're not even saying "excuse me" when you burp. The fourth year you listen to each other like the children listen to Charlie Brown's teacher ("wah-wah-wah"). The fifth year you're either killing each other, filing for divorce, or hopefully, making peace with each other's annoyances and knowing how to resolve conflicts quickly and effectively. We think it takes about five years to work out the kind of kinks in your marriage that'll make a business partnership successful.
2. **Can you play well together?** Sounds like a joke, but it's the most serious question in this chapter. Can you play doubles against another team without

screaming at each other when one of you keeps double faulting on game point? Can you play cards and remain on speaking terms when one of you makes a bone-headed mistake that loses the bet? Here's the point: If you can't play well together what makes you think you can work well together?

3. **Do your business strengths complement or compete?** Somebody has to make the doughnut and somebody has to make the hole. If both of you have complementary skills, you can fit like a puzzle. Clearly, we've oversimplified the problem, but it makes the point: Do you have enough diversity of knowledge and experience that you can work as a team? The most successful working couples we know utilize their different skill sets and have separate areas of responsibility.

Action Step #2

Put the Inc. into your marriage without bankrupting your business or the relationship.

Okay, so you've been married at least five years, you play well together, and your skills are complementary rather than competitive. We say go for it! But not before you make a plan.

Declare where you shine and where you don't. The first step is to forget about the traditional roles you had in previous jobs, as either a homemaker or the breadwinner. Instead, start by looking at blank slates of time–24 hours in a day, 7 days a week. Fill in your optimum times for waking, working, exercise, down time, and eating. Think about these questions: What are your constraints? Do work hours need to correspond to clients' hours or suppliers' hours? Do you have a body rhythm that leads you to being fresher in the morning, afternoon, or evening? Would a 30-minute nap at the right time in the day revive you? If you have children, you'll have definite times that will be devoted to them, but it doesn't have to be the same parent at the same time each day. Determine strengths and weaknesses, likes and dislikes, dreams and nightmares, what bores you and what excites you.

Who does what best? Once you have a good idea of your constraints, you'll need to go over your strengths. Sit down together and answer who is best at the following:

- ➡ Vision and strategy?
- ➡ Operations and tactics?
- ➡ Sales?
- ➡ Customer service?
- ➡ Accounting and finance?
- ➡ Technology?
- ➡ Research and analysis?
- ➡ Creativity and innovation?

Answering these questions will establish lines of authority and expertise. But what if you don't have completely separate areas of expertise? Let's say you're both great at marketing, mediocre at operations, and unenviable at numbers. Then what? How do you decide who does what if neither of you are very good at the what? Negotiation if you're really good at it, is the art of letting someone have your way.

You should negotiate the way you negotiate everything else around the house. For instance, if Husband hates taking the trash out and Wife hates doing the dishes, then switch out. Start by making a list of everything that has to be done and then decide who's going to do it. Remember, this is less about what you want to do than what needs to be done. Worst-case scenario? Share the duties you both hate.

Juggling isn't just a circus act. The work-related responsibilities may be easy to divide, but what about the house, kids, homework, dog, cat, and grocery shopping? Personally, we found that assigning ourselves morning and evening responsibilities worked. The early riser takes care of the kids in the morning–waking them, making breakfast, and driving them to the bus stop. Conversely, the night owl supervises homework and bedtime rituals. Dinner is always a joint effort with food on the table between 5:45 and 6 p.m. so there's plenty of time for relaxation, the kids, and revisiting work if needed.

The Big Point

The Five Golden Rules for Working Couples

Nothing will save you from tough times better than following these Golden Rules:

1. There are no bosses, just partners.
2. Perfection is the enemy of progress.
3. Be thankful your partner isn't like you.
4. Keep your gender-related ego in the closet. There's no place for "women's work" or a "man's job" at Mr. and Mrs. Inc.
5. Shift the load when you see your spouse's routine has gotten more stressful or time-consuming than yours.

Plan, plan, plan. Birds wing it; successful working couples plan it. Don't make the "we'll cross that bridge when we come to it" mistake. Spend a little time on Planet Plan-it before you come down to Earth. Here's what worked for us:

Conduct Morning Reviews

You know those meetings you *hated* at your last job? Well, guess what. You're going to have a lot more of them. Mercifully, they'll be brief and you won't have to suffer with people who just like to hear themselves talk. Start with a brief review of the day's plans. Don't assume you know what your spouse's priorities are for the day. We did our morning review over breakfast. These were typical questions: What does the day look like? Who has meetings outside of the office? What are the big events for the week? Are the kids covered? What's for dinner? Food may seem like an odd thing to bring up at a business meeting, but you're not working at an ordinary business. Take it from us, not having a "food plan" is a disaster waiting to happen. Picture this: It's the end of the day, and you're exhausted and hungry. So are the kids. Each of you assumed the other would take care of dinner. It's 6:30 p.m. and there's nothing on the table, the oven, or the stove. If you're lucky, the only thing you'll throw at each other is dirty looks. Keep the peace and plan the food.

Month-at-a-glance strategies

Document a plan for each week listing any travel, events, meetings, doctors' appointments, school commitments, and anything that will place you as missing in action. We use a pushpin bulletin board in the kitchen or laundry room and install a large monthly calendar listing everyone's activities. Looking out over several weeks has another added advantage: planning your getaways–an essential part of successful businesses we'll talk about in a minute.

Master the Tech

Invest in technologies that will seamlessly provide wireless, phone, e-mail, Web, contacts, and synchronizable calendars. Getting stuck in traffic without client and vendor contacts, family contacts, doctors, or your kids' school contact numbers when something urgent happens will cure you of the thought that you don't need anything but a cell phone. One last thing: laptops are tops! We like them because it liberates us from our home. If you work a lot–and you will if you're successful–you're going to sometimes feel trapped in your home office. Laptops are the keys to opening your mobile world. You can work anywhere–a coffee house, a restaurant, or different parts of the house, such as the living room or backyard.

Action Step #3

Keep the Inc. out of your marriage when home is your office.

The biggest danger of operating a business out of a house is the lack of boundaries. If you're not careful your house will suffer from paperwork creep and chronic machine beeps–the business takes over the house.

Make the rest of your house a business-free zone. Section off your home office and never, ever leave business letters, invoices, cards, or materials laying around other parts of the house. When the fed-ex or UPS truck shows up, take the package straight to the office. Keep the business calls in the business part of the house. Don't let the ringing fax permeate the house–put it on low. We call it our "Keep it Sane" campaign. The home office, similar to any corporate office, is going to be a space filled with stress, deadlines, and anxieties. Don't let it ooze into your home. When you close the home office door, there shouldn't be anything outside of it that reminds you of what's beyond it. We know it's difficult to turn the switch to the off position when you're in the middle of a business crisis, but if you find yourself talking about business in the living room, stop and move into the office. The rest of your home should be a sanctuary–not a satellite office.

Develop a signal to alert your spouse that work is over. We do it with classical music. It's soothing and stress-relieving. Because it's a routine, hearing the music confirms we're out of our business mode and into our married life.

Turn it off, together. Take mini-vacations together. Give your Blackberry a rest. Get a change of scenery; notify your customers in advance. If, for legitimate reasons you need to stay in touch with the business, set aside time each day to check in and make calls. Even though you're not 100-percent free, a break will help, or, turn it off, apart. If they're never apart, even couples who love each other to death end up wanting to kill each other. So, consider taking separate mini-vacations: A day or two at the spa or the golf course, it doesn't matter. When personal space disappears it's time for you to do the same.

Action Step #4

Dig deeper when working with your spouse isn't working.

What do you do when the love of your life turns into the bane of your existence? What do you do if your relationship is growing but the business is tanking? How do you know when it's time to hold on or time to let go? By asking the tough questions and answering them honestly. Here are some of the questions you need to ask yourselves:

- ➡ Have you lost your passion and drive for the business because you've been working with your spouse?
- ➡ Do you secretly long for the "good old days" when you didn't work together?
- ➡ Do your friends, kids, and relatives notice a change for the worse in you?
- ➡ Do arguments with your spouse go unresolved? Do you notice more friction?
- ➡ Do you find every excuse to get out of the office so you don't have to interact with your spouse?

If you answered yes to more questions than you'd like to admit, the next step is to figure out if the situation is salvageable. Just because things are going badly doesn't mean you can't turn it around. If every irritated CEO quit because of turmoil, the economy would collapse.

You know how you feel, but can you identify the underlying problem? Attacking your spouse with, "It's not working out. We can't continue like this," won't help your marriage or your business. But if you can say, "I'm having difficulty with your communication style when we work together. I feel you're always talking down to me," you'll have a greater chance of resolving the problem. We've put together some of the most common problems couples encounter and solutions that should put you back on track:

Problem: Work vs. home personality changes. Your husband's personality went from Jekyll to Hyde once you began working together. Where are those positive qualities you thought would be so helpful to the business?

Solution: It's not unusual that the husband at home can be very different from the husband at work. Here's some familiar "personality" changes and how to address them.

Problem : Unclear roles. You're always tripping over each other at work. You spend hours killing yourself on a business issue only to find out Wife took care of it yesterday. You're arguing about who was supposed to pick up the kids from daycare.

Solution: Astute planning and division of responsibilities will keep you from driving each other crazy. The first task you must complete as Mr. and Mrs. Inc. is determining who does what. Remember, you'll both be juggling work and personal priorities, so follow our golden rule and keep your gender-related ego in the closet. Then, create a standing schedule for the week ahead that includes the business and personal activities. Review the day's priorities the night before or in the morning. Don't forget to cover your partner's back when they are carrying a heavy load.

Problem: Unrealistic expectations. You thought your spouse could move easily from a larger organization, only to find out they can't function without a staff. You were anticipating that Spouse would significantly increase sales in the first 90 days, but he or she didn't. You thought you'd make money right away, but you're losing it instead.

Solution: Sounds as though you may be the problem, and showing your disappointment is a good way of having a short career together. You have the obligation to help your new partner make the adjustment. Your expectations for growth and success are probably right, so add patience, lower the pressure, and encourage your spouse.

Problem: You're suffocating each other. Your home office turned into a home prison and you can't find a warden to let you out. You're pining for a home life and some personal space.

Solution: If you can't expand your work area, consider alternating work hours and taking separate lunches so that you and you spouse have the office to yourselves at different times. Other wise, pick up your laptop and do some tasks off-site, whether it's the local coffee house or the library.

What he's like at home	**What he's like at the office**	**Solution**
Helpful and cheerful. Ask him to do something and he's on it. He's confident you can do your thing without a babysitter.	A control freak that constantly checks your progress; competitive with how your responsibilities compare to his.	Remind him that he's not working with the Alpha Dogs at his old company and you have no intention of taking his bone! You made this move to make a better life.
Like a guest at a hotel: he leaves his towels and newspapers on the floor. He acts like he's a paying customer.	Each night he takes all of his papers off his desk, straightens his chair and desk. He then crticizes you for not being orderly.	Tell him you respect the way he keeps his area and promise to be more orderly at the office, but he also needs to promise to be cleaner around the house.
He has a warm, loving tone. He suggests what he wants ina way that makes it easy to agree.	Barking out orders and being compulsively urgent, he adds to the stress of your day.	Ask why he needs to be so unpleasant. He has to recognize that working together is about a better life, and he needs to try harder.

Chapter Summary

Mr. and Mrs. Inc.

The biggest challenge Mr. and Mrs. Inc. face is growing the business without shrinking their marriage. Whether you're working together or considering it, here's a summary of our Action Steps learned from personal experience.

- **Action Step #1:** Your chances of success will be greater if you've been married at least five years, you play well together, and your skills are complementary.
- **Action Step #2:** Follow our plan to get the Mr. and Mrs. Inc. collaboration off to a good start:
  - Determine each other's strengths and weaknesses.
  - Assign responsibilities.
  - Learn to juggle work and household responsibilities.
  - Make planning an integral part of your life together.
  - Invest in the technology that makes life together as Mr. and Mrs. Inc. easier.
- **Action Step #3:** Don't let the business overrun your marriage when your office is in your home.
- **Action Step #4:** Dig deeper when working with your spouse isn't working.

Chapter 11

The Perplexed Parent

"That someday has arrived son - it's all yours."

Which is worse: hearing your kids say, "How could you do this to us?" or hearing your accountant say, "How could you do this to yourself?" Either way, deciding whether to sell the family business or give it to the kids is one of the toughest decisions a parent can make, especially when you think the business has some tough challenges ahead or you don't think the kids are strong enough to run the company.

So, do you hand the business to the kids and take the chance they will scramble your nest egg? Or do you sell the business and take a chance they'll never speak to you again?

If you are a Perplexed Parent, this chapter will help you figure out whether you're better off keeping or selling the business. We'll walk you through a series of questions that will identify the important factors. Then we'll give you a step-by-step way to bring your family into the decision-making process without alienating anyone. Keep in mind that the challenge you face isn't an either/or proposition. There are alternatives you may not have thought about, and we'll go over them in detail. Finally, if you decide to sell the business, we'll share some of the secrets we learned in selling two family businesses.

If you're not a Perplexed Parent but you're dealing with one, this chapter will help you understand them better and help them think through the decision rationally. We'll start with a common scenario, provide some insights, and move on to recommendations.

The Perplexed Parent's Dilemma: A Typical Scenario

Should I hand the business to my kids or sell it?

It's decision time. Retirement is around the corner, but what's in the future–prosperity or the poorhouse? It all depends on whether handing the business to the kids will be the smartest or dumbest thing I'll ever do.

There is no black-and-white answer. In the past, the business always provided good cash flow, but lately sales projections look anemic, and the entire industry seems to need a transfusion. My sons think I'm being too pessimistic about the future, but I'm not so sure.

Maybe I'm more pessimistic about "them" running the business than the business itself. If only I felt confident they could work well together. Just yesterday, my older son missed a proposal deadline because his brother didn't provide the pricing and references on time. Was it intentional? Who knows? Everybody has a great excuse.

I was bursting with pride when both boys joined the business. At first, everything was great. But as we got bigger, their testosterone kicked in and one-upmanship became an everyday occurrence. Today, they seem more interested in building their fiefdoms than growing our profits. Sometimes I think they actually enjoy watching each other fail.

I talked to my lawyer and he's definitely in the "sell" camp. "Foreign companies are paying top dollar for smaller companies like yours," he said. "They've got the latest technology and you don't. They've also got something else you don't."

"Oh, yeah?" I said. "What?"

"Executives that can work together." I guess everyone knows about the boys.

My lawyer may be in the "sell" camp, but my wife sure isn't. She went ballistic when I told her. "How could you do this to the boys?" she said. You brought them into the business and now you're pulling the rug out from underneath them! Did you even give them enough time to prove themselves?" Then she voiced my biggest fear of all. "They'll be so angry," she said, "they'll probably move just so we'll never see the grandchildren."

I know she's right. The boys would be devastated if I sold the business. Just when I think I have the answer, I go back to square one. Do I take the risk the boys will run the business into the ground, or sell it and take the risk our relationship will never be the same? I don't know which is worse–being a Wal-Mart greeter at age 65 or being alone at 70. Whatever I choose, I lose.

What's the Perplexed Parent Thinking?

Mr. & Mrs. Perplexed are so anxious they're making their coffee nervous. Do they take the money and run or take a chance and go bust? Do they protect themselves financially and risk a family meltdown? Or do they deed the business to the kids and risk a financial meltdown?

It's easy to see why the Perplexed Parent is so confused. The family may interpret what should be a rational business decision as cold-hearted betrayal. Or, at the very least, a dramatic flip-flop–the one that pushed cousin Jenny over the edge. The battle between financial security and perpetuating the family legacy becomes a Rubik's Cube of questions, what-ifs, and emotions. It's not just about the business–if that isn't enough to cause gray hair. The Perplexed Parent has to evaluate the family's capabilities, their ability to work together, choosing a successor, and Parent's own financial security. Might as well add everyone's favorite relative, Uncle Sam, to the pile, because Parent has to consider the tax impact of all the options. Top it off with the dismal statistics about family businesses surviving into the next generation and you're calling the doctor for that Prozac prescription!

It's enough to make anyone have a panic attack. The Perplexed Parent feels certainty one day and confusion the next. After all, how do you tell your kids you're selling the company because you don't have enough faith in them? How do you tell them that your financial security is more important than the family legacy you encouraged them to embrace since they were kids?

We know, because we faced those questions, too. In our case, the company's product became a commodity, profit margins were down, the company's growth had outpaced our management skills, and family relationships were moving in the wrong direction. We could have used a blueprint–a guide to help us determine the best course of action. We didn't, but you do (you're holding it).

First, let's make a frank, systematic assessment of your family and your business. When it comes to keeping or selling your business, we don't know the answers, but we do know the questions. Then, whichever way you're leaning, we'll show you how to bring the family into the decision-making process to help minimize any destructive fallout. If you decide to keep the business in the family, we'll give you some appealing, but not-so-obvious, alternatives to discuss with your advisors. Finally, if you do decide to sell, we'll provide you with a series of secrets we learned after selling two family businesses.

Five Action Steps for the Perplexed Parent

Action Step #1

Can your family cut it? Take the test.

Weigh the two critical factors: the family's competence and compatibility. A family business can't have one without the other if it's to survive and thrive. Does your family have the street smarts to push the company forward? The intellectual capacity to consider multiple factors before making decisions? The ability to anticipate and adapt to changes? If the answer's yes, great. But that's only half the equation. What good are street smarts if Son and his sister can't resolve conflicts successfully? What good is brainpower if Daughter likes making everyone else in the family look stupid? "Plays well with others" isn't just a report card comment; it's a must in family business. Figure out where your family stands by considering the following questions. Answer honestly and you're well on your way to making the right decision.

- ➠ What's the track record? Are family members more often right than wrong when it comes to business decisions?
- ➠ Do you believe they have a good feel for the industry and its challenges? Do you have confidence in their ability to meet the challenges?
- ➠ Do the company's key employees respect them as leaders?
- ➠ Have they met benchmarks set by you or them?
- ➠ Are family members passionate about the business?
- ➠ Do they feel the sense of purpose so critical in family business survival?
- ➠ Are they self-starters?
- ➠ Do you trust their judgment?

If you've answered no to the competency questions more than you would prefer, don't panic; at least not yet. Sometimes a question about competency just can't be answered today. For example, do your children show promise but have no management track record because they're too young or inexperienced?

Or, have you preferred to be the sole decision-maker and not really given them the opportunity to prove themselves?

If you've come to the inescapable conclusion that you're better off selling the business than leaving it to the kids, don't feel bad. Thousands of family business owners came to the same conclusion and sold the business with their families and financial futures intact. Move on to Action Step #3 to learn how to break the news without breaking your bonds.

If you've answered yes to most of the questions, and feel your family's competency isn't an issue, you're still not out of the woods. They may be competent but are they compatible? If they don't get along, the best team in the industry can be the worst thing for the business. Answer the following:

- Can your family resolve business squabbles? (Or are you always the referee with the whistle?)
- Is there teamwork among family members?
- When something goes wrong, does the family work together to fix it or do they play the blame game?
- Do family members seem to get along at social events? Or do they find ingenious ways to avoid each other?
- Do they initiate social get-togethers on their own?
- Can you name three instances where sibling rivalries or other jealousies were handled well and didn't interfere with the business for very long?
- Do you believe that the family works well together and enjoys the challenge of working in a family business?

Several no's mean that the family part of the family business isn't working. We don't mean to be pessimistic, but in our experience, a lack of competency is easier to fix than a lack of compatibility. Your only hope for turning bad blood into good business is detailed in Action Step #3. Good luck!

The Big Point

Competence and compatibility are two sides of the same coin. You can't leave the company to bright kids who don't get along anymore than you can leave it to kids who love each other but couldn't find the net income line on a profit and loss statement (P&L) if their life depended on it.

Action Step #2

Assess the company and the industry. Is it thriving or diving?

You may have the best team in the world, but if you're in a dying industry, they're not going to do you much good. You could go into another industry, but really, that's another book. Answer the following questions and figure out where you stand.

If you answered yes more than you'd prefer, it may be time to take the money and run. Move on to the next step to learn how you should present your conclusion to the rest of the family.

- Are you seeing a downward trend in sales and profits?
- Has your borrowing increased significantly on your working capital loan?
- Will the company require a financial investment to update its processes, production capabilities, and other assets?

- If so, are you concerned about signing on the line for these commitments (and/or reducing your draw from the business)?
- Do you need a human resource pruning to improve the efficiency and cost structure?
- Are you against paying out big dollars to terminate staff members who will be entitled to severance packages?

Action Step #3

To sell or not to sell? That is the question (for everyone).

Making a unilateral decision is the one thing we guarantee will rip your family apart. Go it alone and you'll end up alone for the rest of your life, or until someone forgives you, whichever comes first.

If your style is to keep your cards close to the vest, you better learn how to show them. The severity of the family's reaction to an unpopular decision is in direct proportion to the Perplexed Parent's silence in making it. What you consider a private way of reaching a decision they'll think of as a treacherous vote of no confidence. Once the news sets in, shock and disappointment will progress to anger toward you: Weren't you the one that coaxed your daughter into joining the family business in the first place? Didn't you mislead your son when you said he'd be president someday? Aren't you responsible for putting your niece back in the job market? Leave the surprises to birthday parties. They have no place in high-voltage decisions.

Remember, sharing the decision-making process is not the same thing as sharing the decision. Make no mistake about it, *you,* the Perplexed Parent will make the decision. But you can weigh the options alone and alienate almost everyone, or ask for input and isolate almost no one.

Let the Conversation Begin

Do you need a blueprint for conveying the news? After the experience of witnessing both good and bad deliveries, we've put together some pointers we think will work best:

Pick the right time and place

Make calls to relevant family members on a Thursday night or Friday for a weekend meeting at your house. Tell them you want to discuss an important family issue, but don't want to give any details before the meeting. Why the short notice? Less time for anxiety to rattle everyone's nerves. Why the weekend? To let the emotions simmer down before the workweek ahead. Remember, the last thing you want is an emotional outburst as your family leaves your office during work hours.

Prepare, prepare, prepare

After you've been through the questions in Action Steps #1 and #2, get your big ideas on paper. Solicit input from advisors, a close friend who can keep it confidential, or your spouse. Then frame the points into an appropriate conversation with the family. What do we mean? Let's say your answers on the competency section reveal you're better off selling. We don't want you to tell your family you don't have confidence in them. That's a blow rarely deserved. Instead, frame that point by saying, "The future challenges in this industry are so great, I think we'll all be better off if we sell while we have a valuable company." No finger pointing. No hurt feelings.

Be sure to bring the latest reports showing the status of the company and the industry–financial statements and trends, market analysis and market share, and industry forecasts and recent articles identifying troublesome issues.

However, if your sales are up and the future looks bright, but you're convinced the family can't manage it, discuss bringing in a professional manager with a proven track record. Tell them the pro can teach them more than you can. He'll protect the business and be a mentor for the family. With luck, he or she will prepare them for a more significant role while preserving the golden goose. This plan will give you more time to see if you'll need that for sale sign.

Lead with your heart, not your wallet

Begin by conveying your anguish over the decision of whether or not to sell the business. You never wanted to be in this position, but circumstances have forced your hand. If you've had physical symptoms or even depression, discuss it openly. Let them know the emotional affect this situation has had on you (and your spouse), and that selling the business wasn't in the plans but it now must be considered.

The facts and nothing but the facts

Start with the truth as you see it–the factors and criteria that you believe are important in the decision-making process. Go over the points you've identified in Action Steps #1 and 2. If the concern is primarily the health and future of the company, let it all hang out: the financials, the trends, your position in the market, rumors about competitors, the industry. Describe your concerns about the business and the risk involved if additional debt is required to revamp existing operations.

If you've hit a significant roadblock in the industry, and feel as though there are significant challenges to which you don't want to invest the money, be upfront with your family.

When the family needs a time-out

If the family's ability to work together is a concern, have each family member answer the previous compatibility questions. Then, open the discussion with this line: "It's clear that we've got a great team that doesn't work well together. What can we all do to reverse the test results and make it possible to continue our family legacy?" They need to hear loud and clear that you will take action and the status quo is not acceptable. You could, of course, be opening Pandora's box, but we think it's worth it. Here's why: You're giving them fair warning about what's going to happen. If you decide to sell, they will not be blindsided; you've given them the opportunity to turn things around.

Bring up your retirement

Tell the family that you're not going to lead the business forever and that your financial security is an important component to the decision. You don't have to get into facts and figures, but you can discuss your expectations and how the decision affects it.

The next steps

Unless everyone walked out on you, your goal is to end the meeting with a plan. Here are two possibilities:

1. **A word from the wise: Engage a financial advisor or consultant to explore your options.** We've pointed out some alternatives to discuss with them in the next section. Keep the family

calm with regular updates. Try to let the family attend the meetings so decisions are transparent and they see the process firsthand.

2. **Bring in the family therapist.** Did everyone agree that the family has been more of a problem than the business? Are they committed to changing the way they relate to each other? Put some parameters around the promises by bringing a family therapist or consultant on board. Make sure there's a timetable to chart progress and schedule a family follow-up in three to six months.

Whatever the choice you make, stress to the family the importance of keeping the discussions private. If employees or customers hear rumors the company is for sale before you're prepared with your story, it could be disastrous.

The point of all this is to give your family input into the decision. By handling things sensitively but firmly, you'll minimize the damage of a "sell" decision and maximize the goodwill of a "legacy" decision. If you handle this *very* well, your kids will know what your decision is before you do.

Action Step #4

Learn about other options.

Don't assume you're limited to a sell or no-sell option. There are other alternatives between keeping the status quo and selling 100 percent of the company. Here are a few:

- Let the family purchase the company from you. If your family wants to continue in the business and you don't, they can purchase all or part of your stock (if you're willing to keep a stake in the company). This can be an attractive alternative when one of your goals is to beef up your nest egg. There are numerous ways to accomplish this and any good advisor can recommend whether private equity investors, an ESOP, or a friendly banker is your answer.

- Sell the company, bank some money, and start or buy a smaller business. If your family works well together, get a fresh start. Cash out, bank some proceeds, and invest in another manageable, promising business. It can be in the same industry (as long as you don't violate your noncompete) or a new one where a transfer of skills and renewed purpose could rally the family together in a way the old business couldn't.
- Merge with a competitor. If the industry is hammering you, you're not alone. A merger may solve some of the problems; look for a combination that takes advantage of synergies and eliminates redundancies. For example, did your competitor in the next state install a software system that you wanted but could never afford? Do you have a senior management they always wanted but couldn't attract? Is your geography complimentary to theirs? If you feel like you're in hell, a marriage might make it heaven.

The Big Point

Bring in the Big Guns

Relying on Uncle Henry to guide you through the complex world of mergers, acquisitions, and other financial transactions is not a good idea. Hire a law firm and accounting firm that specializes in these transactions. A broker or investment banker can help you manage the deal, especially when you're exploring several options and have multiple shareholders.

Action Step #5

Caution! Avoid the landmines in the selling process.

Once you decide to sell the family business, your life will turn upside down. Even the best juggler will have his hands full keeping investment bankers, lawyers, accountants, employees, and customers from knocking into each other in mid-air. After going through the process twice, we want to share some of the little-known secrets of selling a family business.

If you think you work hard now...

The selling process is an enormous undertaking: lengthy, offsite meetings with advisors and potential buyers; preparing financial information; gathering every legal document and client contract since the beginning of time. Putting out fires that erupt in the rumor mill will take up most of your day. You will need to reassign some of your duties to others. Do you need to be at every management meeting? Can you send another manager to see a client? Can you get your doctor to double your prescription?

Get ready for M&A buzzwords, capitals gains, and eyestrains

What's an "add back"? Welcome to the world of earnings before interest, taxes, depreciation, and amortization (EBITDA); asset and stock sales; due diligence; capital gains; and legal representations. You should get a good attorney, tax specialist, or investment banker who can explain everything. You may know a lot about running your business, but selling is a completely different animal. Get familiar with the basics before the process begins, so you won't have to play catch-up.

The Big Point

Why You Should Hire A Pro

Your advisors are worth their weight in gold. When the buyer is overreaching on a critical point, an experienced advisor knows the market standards. Let him or her negotiate those contentious terms and conditions. Some common problem areas are payment terms, collateral, representations and warranties, and work agreements.

Rent your controller's silence and loyalty

Your controller will be working overtime, generating reams of financial information. It won't be long before they figure out it's not business as usual. *Tell them the truth.* And while you're at it, buy his or her cooperation by paying a retention bonus if they stay until the company is sold. With all the banking, accounting, and administrative details to iron out, it's money well spent. Also, pay a bonus for any extra hours worked producing the financial schedules and administrative information. Bring in temporary help if the work is overwhelming and you don't want the remaining staff to know what's going on.

Honesty is not the best policy

Telling everyone the truth about your plans isn't the way to go. Speculation and rumors will spiral out of control with employees, and possibly customers, jumping ship. Prepare the company story and share it with your inner circle. Expect customers to question you directly about your plans. A possible answer: "The kids are interested in buying the company and we're talking to a private equity group. This was always part of our plan, and we have to pull together a lot of information."

Remember, you'll also need a story to cover all the information requests at the office; for example, the company is getting prepared for the audit early this year; the company is getting new financing and needs five-year projections.

Golden handcuffs for the A team

You don't want important customers deserting you. Make your executives feel secure with a generous severance agreement or retention bonus. If they're your best people, your competitors would love to hire them.

Get ready, get set, get nervous

Good days, great days, bad days, mad days–that's what your week will be like. You won't feel comfortable until you've closed the deal. We suggest buying some antacid by the case.

You will lose control of confidential information

Your most confidential information will be on the table including any "special situations" you may have had. Even when a potential buyer signs a confidentiality agreement, information is copied, left open in someone's office, or inadvertently shown to someone not covered by the agreement. What could wind up in the wrong hands? Customer names and contract information, details about products or services, operating results by line and geography, all human resource and salary specifics, and anything else you attempt to keep private.

When negotiating, get the big points out of the way first

"Time is of the essence" isn't just a contractual term. Once you're in negotiations, time is not on your side. You're in danger of losing employees and customers everyday that goes by. Don't waste time with a buyer who can't satisfy an important point. Some deal breakers to get out of the way: payment terms, collateral, future employment of family or key managers, disposition of liabilities; earn-out provisions. Your advisors should help you keep up the pressure to close. Remember, if your deal doesn't close after months of negotiating, other potential buyers will see blood in the water.

If the deal fails, damage control is job number-one

There aren't enough compasses to show how many deals have gone south. Do not assume that genuine interest and an investment in due diligence will result in signed contracts. What will you do if it fails?

Brace yourself for an extensive "road show"; you'll need to visit customers personally. Tell them that after exploring different options, you've decided to keep the status quo. Calm down the office in the same way by meeting with your key managers. They may ask you for financial guarantees and employment agreements. Remember, your immediate goal is to stabilize the company and make the recent uncertainty a fading memory. You'll be met with distrust and will need to reattach the bond where possible, but expect it to take time.

And after the sale? You're still not done!

Selling the business doesn't mean you can take an extended vacation the next day. You'll probably be on full-time duty for the next six months to a year with a variety of transition issues. Except for the money in the bank, you may forget you've even sold the business–until you get a call from "the boss" you never had. In our experience with both stock and asset sales, the asset sale had the longest afterlife, because it requires months of closing down the corporation, paying bills, collecting money, and resolving old issues.

Finally, when things wind down, you'll look back and be amazed that you got through it. Now, you'll have a badge of honor showing you're a member of a private club comprised of other family business owners that sold their businesses also. What war stories you'll share!

Chapter Summary

The Perplexed Parent

Here's a summary of the five Action Steps we've given you to determine whether you should hand the business to your kids or sell it.

- **Action Step #1:** Take the test to see if your family can handle the business. They must be compatible AND competent.
- **Action Step #2:** Next, determine if your company and the industry are thriving or diving.
- **Action Step #3:** Bring in your family to hear your assessment of where they and the company stand. You make the ultimate decision, but include them in the process.
- **Action Step #4:** Learn about other options. Don't assume you are limited to a "sell-no sell" option.
- **Action Step #5:** Avoid the landmines in the selling process. Read our little-known secrets learned after going through the process with two companies.

Conclusion

Thanks for spending time with some or all of the characters in this book. We hope they've helped you come to a better understanding of the characters in your own family business. And more importantly, how to deal with them to everyone's satisfaction.

There are a few things we'd like you to keep in mind before you put the book on the shelf:

1. **Your family business is unique, but your problems aren't.** Whether Dad the Decider won't relinquish his throne, the Sibling Rivals use the office as their battlefield, or Uncle Ben's remarriage rockets everyone to the moon, all family businesses go through the same conflicts and challenges. Don't be embarrassed or surprised. You are not alone.
2. **Act now so you're not disappointed later.** Family-based problems won't disappear with time. In fact, they'll get bigger and uglier, so don't ignore them. Think like a physician—early detection and treatment gets the best results.

3. **Breaking news!** Everyone in the family is in the family business. Even if you don't work in it, you're affected by it. Everyone shares in the rewards and the misery. So, even though you might despise your new daughter-in-law or the brother who doesn't work in the business, they will affect it. Relationships always do. Keep the peace and you'll grow the business.
4. **Call in the cavalry.** Don't let embarrassment, ego, or expense keep you from hiring family business consultants or talking to a therapist. If you want to keep the business on track, remember the old saying: "You're the only one who can do it, but you can't do it alone."
5. **Everyone in the family should treat the business with the respect it deserves.** That means not using it as the family ATM or the career choice of last resort for that irresponsible niece. That means protecting it from the family's misadventures in love. Respect has a way of preventing a lot of problems, so cultivate it early and often.

In closing, we want to offer one last piece of advice: Use *Family Inc.* the way you'd use a dictionary or a thesaurus–as a reference book you keep going back to when you want to get something right or find a better way to handle it. Here's why: Every time you think you've graduated from the school of experience somebody in your family will think up a new course, so use this book as a way of graduating from whatever they throw at you.

Thank you for giving us the privilege of helping you keep your family in the business. For more information, you can contact us at authors@familyincbook.com.

Bibliography

Allen, Elaine I. and Nas S. Langowitz. "Women in Family-Owned Business." Center for Women's Leadership at Babson College and Mass Mutual Financial Group, August 2003.

Aronoff, Craig E., Joseph H. Astrachan, and John L. Ward. *Making Sibling Teams Work: the Next Generation.* Marietta, Ga.: Family Enterprise Publishers, 1997.

Astrachan, Joseph H., Kristi S. McMillan. *Conflict and Communication in the Family Business.* Marietta, Ga.: Family Enterprise Publishers, 2003.

Fleming, Quentin J. *Keep the Family Baggage Out of the Family Business.* New York: Fireside, 2000.

Frankenberg, Ellen. *Your Family, Inc.* Binghamton, New York: Haworth Press, 1999.

Galloni, Alessandra Galloni. "At 168, the House of Hermes ponders its fashion future." The Wall Street Journal, March 7, 2005.

Gersick, Kelin E., John A. Davis, Marion Hampton, and Ivan Lansberg. *Generation to Generation.* Boston, Massachusetts: Harvard Business School Press, 1997.

Hoover, Edwin A., and Colette Lombard Hoover. *Getting Along in Family Business.* New York and London: Routledge, 1999.

Horn, Robert. "The Families That Own Asia–Thailand." Time Asia, February 23, 2004.

Nicholson, Nigel, and Asa Bjornberg. *Family Business Leadership Inquiry*. United Kingdom: Institute for Family Business, 2005.

Paisner, Marshall B. *Sustaining the Family Business.* Cam bridge, Massachusetts: Basic Books, 1999.

Pitts, Gordon. *In the Blood.* Canada: Doubleday Canada, 2000.

Saritha Rai. "India Shares Rally as a Family Feud Ends," New York Times, June 21, 2005.

Schuman, Michael. "The Families That Own Asia–Taiwan." Time Asia, February 23, 2004.

Ward, John L. *Perpetuating the Family Business.* Houndmills, Basingstoke, Hampshire and New York: Palgrave McMillan, 2004.

Websites

www.thestar.com.my/news/story/2007/6/23/bizweek. "YTL Corp Tan Sri Yeoh Tiang Lay." By: Anita Gabriel and Tee Lin Say, December 4, 2007.

www.taipeitimes.com/news/world/archives/2007/06/12. "South Korea: Rich dad wants son-in-law," August 6, 2007.

www.economist.com/people displayStory.cfm?story_id=3599327. "Breaking into a man's world," January 10, 2007.

www.ffi.org/genTemplate.asp?cid=186. "Facts and Perspectives on Family Businesses Around the World," December 9, 2007.

Index

Larry Colin is a 37-year veteran of the 92-year-old family business, Colin Service Systems, Inc. From an entry-level position in his grandfather's small window-cleaning company, he became president, CEO, and ultimately, chairman, of the facilities support services company. Larry helped build the company into two multi-state enterprises, including Effective Security Systems, with 10,000 employees and sales approaching $200 million. On December 22, 2004, Colin Service was sold to a large publicly traded competitor.

Larry and the family business have been featured on CNBC and in Crain's New York. Quoted in the best-seller *1001 Ways to Reward Employees,* Larry has been a guest speaker at trade associations on a variety of business topics including mergers and acquisitions, customer service, and business development.

Laura Colin graduated from Northwestern University's J.L. Kellogg Graduate School of Business. After completing the program, she moved to New York City to work as an investment banker at Salomon Brothers and in economic development in North Africa. Laura subsequently worked in Larry's family business, both part-time and later full-time. As vice president of finance, she played a major role in selling the company in 2004.